Praise for
FOCUS FORWARD

"I have always believed that motorsports—especially endurance sportscar racing—teaches invaluable life lessons to all who participate. In *Focus Forward*, Ted Giovanis has done a masterful job of bringing this to life."

JOHN DOONAN, President, International Motor Sports Association

"I've greatly benefited from *Focus Forward*'s wisdom about everyday life, which is delivered by a tenacious competitor, a deep thinker, and a razor-sharp student of sportscar racing."

HUGH PLUMB, professional race car driver and Team TGM general manager

"Motor racing needs application, dedication, and an unusual blend of forward-planning, reading the situation, and super-quick decision-making. In *Focus Forward*, Ted Giovanis reveals how this recipe provides results in all aspects of life away from the track."

JOHN HINDHAUGH, broadcaster and founder of Radio Show Limited, which airs over 7,000 hours of live motorsports annually

FOCUS FORWARD

www.amplifypublishinggroup.com

Focus Forward: Life Lessons from Racing

For more information, please contact:
Amplify, an imprint of Amplify Publishing Group
620 Herndon Parkway, Suite 220
Herndon, VA 20170
info@amplifypublishing.com

Library of Congress Control Number: 2023906601
CPSIA Code: PRV0523
ISBN-13: 978-1-63755-503-3
Printed in the United States

To my daughters,

Allie and Kristina

FOCUS
FORWARD

LIFE LESSONS
FROM RACING

TED GIOVANIS

amplify
an imprint of Amplify Publishing Group

"It is not the critic who counts; not the man who points out how the strong man stumbles, or where the doer of deeds could have done them better. The credit belongs to the man who is actually in the arena, whose face is marred by dust and sweat and blood; who strives valiantly; who errs, who comes short again and again, because there is no effort without error and shortcoming; but who does actually strive to do the deeds; who knows great enthusiasms, the great devotions; who spends himself in a worthy cause; who at the best knows in the end the triumph of high achievement, and who at the worst, if he fails, at least fails while daring greatly, so that his place shall never be with those cold and timid souls who neither know victory nor defeat."

Theodore Roosevelt

Contents

FOREWORD

A successful businessman drawn by the allure of sportscar racing is hardly something new. I've seen it more than once in my twenty-five-plus years in global sports broadcasting. In fact, it's the lifeblood of this category of motorsport. There is a simple two-tier system in sportscar racing: manufacturer-supported organizations and pro-am teams. The latter is what bolsters the sport, as manufacturer involvement ebbs and flows while the pro-am groups are invariably here to stay.

Enter Ted Giovanis. He's a successful businessman not only enticed by the thrill of sportscar racing, but now increasingly more intrigued and motivated by what it takes to succeed in auto racing beyond shiny cars and iconic brands.

I have always been amazed when I meet the next "gentleman or amateur driver" who has the literal drive to race. While these individuals clearly have the financial freedom to sit on a beach in the Bahamas or tour Tuscany sipping wine, they choose to sweat it out at a racetrack—trying to shave another second off a lap time while absorbing every word of advice delivered by their pro partner.

If you haven't yet read Ted's first book *Beyond Fear*, it reveals why he continues to race in the IMSA WeatherTech Sportscar Championship and Michelin Pilot Challenge—against some of the biggest names in racing. He knows he'll never be one of those guys, and he's not trying to be. But then again, he's never been afraid of a fight. It's not often you meet someone who has sued the federal government of the United States and won!

I'm not suggesting for a second that racing sportscars is as daunting as going toe-to-toe with the government, but it's no walk in the park either. *Focus Forward* details what has fascinated Ted and kept him coming back for more. The parallels between business and racing are numerous. The required skill, dedication, decisiveness, and motivation is strikingly similar to that of a company leader.

Over decades, an eclectic collection of CEOs, Chairmen, COOs, inventors, and flat-out crooks have passed through the sport of sportscar racing. But only a few have the genuine passion to try to conquer what they began long ago at a small track somewhere—participating in an invitational drive day or lead-follow session. Ted Giovanis is one of those.

If you're like me, you have a love for all sports. But just because we love golf doesn't mean we can tee up beside Rory McIlroy at Augusta National at The Masters. Sportscar racing is different. Ted Giovanis can be on the same starting grid at the Rolex 24 at Daytona as Scott Dixon, a six-time IndyCar champion and Helio Castroneves, a four-time Indianapolis 500 winner. In and of itself, that's mind-blowing.

This discipline of motor racing is more inclusive than exclusive. The nature of the cars, in comparison to others, is more forgiving and there's the beauty of having at least one co-driver (there are more co-drivers at the longer duration events). It's a fabulous team environment, one that nurtures encouragement and improvement. Ted has the benefit of being surrounded by sportscar veteran drivers Owen Trinkler, Hugh and Matt Plumb, and legendary strategist and Director of Competition Joe Varde. Their combined experience, coupled with Ted's tenacity, has placed this 77-year-old at a level in the sport no one could have thought possible.

Focus Forward tells you what he's learned from the experience—and provides valuable life lessons along the way.

Leigh Diffey
NBC Sports
Host and Commentator—Olympics and Motorsport

INTRODUCTION

The purpose of this book is to outline the parallels between automobile racing and life. While these parallels may seem far-fetched, there are several direct relationships. As such, this book is intended to be a guide to life. I firmly believe that everything I've needed to know in life I learned from racing. It has been an expert guide for navigating everything that happens, day in and day out. I have learned countless lessons from racing, and in this book I have attempted to put them in the context of racing and apply them to real-life situations.

The sections that follow are separated merely for identification. They are intended to progress to a conclusion and that progress is guided by the order of the sections. The order is not intended to imply a hierarchy—they are just part of the progression.

Each chapter begins with one or more quotes. These quotes are intended to set up the reader for what follows. The book's main message is to stay involved, keep progressing, and constantly move forward.

Now, let us begin—enjoy.

1

Racing and Driving: More Complicated Than You Think

"There are only three sports—bullfighting, motor racing, and mountaineering; all the rest are merely games."

Ernest Hemingway

Driving a racecar is not as simple as one might think. I started doing it in 1991, when I was forty-six years old. I thought I was young; I thought I had received some good instruction. I was wrong. At the time, safety underpinned my on-track training. But my instructors did not teach me about the philosophical approach to driving a racecar fast, nor did they say much about handling characteristics, their causes, and their solutions. I am going to briefly review the conceptual view of racing and driving racecars fast. This background will help you understand and absorb the lessons I've learned from racing that can be applied to our lives—mine included.

RACING 101

Most folks view the driving of racecars as being primarily about managing how power is applied and the timing related to that process. Wrong!

Power application and its timing are absolutely part of driving racing cars fast. But the most important part involves *weight and weight management.* The bottom part of each tire—the part in contact with the ground—is referred to as the *contact patch.* There are four such patches and each one is about the size of two size-9 shoes placed together side by side (about 96 square inches). These four 96-square-inch patches control what happens to the car and how it handles. These contact patches, which have a finite amount of grip, can turn, stop, and apply power. Driving a racecar fast involves "feeling" how the weight rests on these four corners. From there, you need to understand how each action you take as a driver influences what the car does, where it goes, and at what speed.

There is a balance to managing what is happening at the contact patches. If we place too much weight on the front tires—by braking heavily—then the car will not turn when we want it to. Conversely, if we shift weight off the front tires—by adding too much power upon exiting a corner—the car will not turn either (the front tires need some weight on them to get them to turn). This is what I mean by *weight management.*

There are driving techniques that come into play here. On a racetrack, the *line* is the theoretical, classic line around the track (think of it as the typical route). Approaching a right-hand turn, one starts on the far left, then turns in, then touches the *apex* of the turn on the right, and then proceeds to track out on the far left exiting the turn. (The term *track out* refers to the point at which, in this hypothetical right-hand turn, you are back on the far left of the track.) This process shortens the turn's radius, which allows for faster speed through the turn or corner. That leads to a faster lap time, which is the objective in driving. This process also involves the change of the line based on the turn's design characteristic, which can vary by corner and by track. More on this later.

The turns on each track vary, which challenges drivers and their cars. When taking a turn there is first the turn-in, where the arc of the turn begins. One must approach the turn gradually, as a smooth arc, not at a specific point. The driver needs to look at the apex of the turn almost before beginning the turn-in, which allows the arc to flow. I look at this process as being akin to art rather than painting by number. The artist lets the brush flow rather than getting to a specific point and then turning the brush in another direction.

Once the apex is achieved, the driver can begin the power application—getting back to throttle. This is usually progressive, but the objective is to get to full power as soon as possible, since being at full throttle longer will yield faster lap times. Finally, there is the *track out* point.

Therefore, our path is far left (turn-in), far right (apex), and now far left again (track out). This path shortens the arc or radius, which is the fastest way through the corner. Ultimately you see racecars drive over the inside or exit curbing, which also changes the radius and contributes to faster corner speeds.

There are *three types of turns*—Type 1, Type 2, and Type 3. A Type 1 turn leads onto the longest straightaway. The straights are the stretches to achieve maximum speed. Type 1 turns are themselves prioritized by the length of the flowing straight. Type 2 turns lead off the straightaways. In approaching these turns, you want to maximize the higher speed achieved on the straight, as this makes it possible to maintain that speed longer. You want to brake as late as possible without sacrificing the corner entry. Maintaining 1 mph longer might come out to two or three car lengths, which is a lot of track space. Type 3 turns are turns between turns. The most important portion of a Type 3 turn is the final one (essentially a Type 1 turn) that leads onto a straight, and the next most important portion is the first, which likely came off a straight. Some of these Type 3 turns can be what's known as "through away" turns, where you could sacrifice speed to maximize the Type 1 turn that follows.

To summarize, the *change in radius of a turn increases the ability to achieve a faster corner speed.* The shorter the radius, the shorter the distance. Corner speed translates directly to lower lap times. The faster the corner speed, the faster the lap time.

Further complicating matters is the *camber* or slope of the track surface. It can be negative (slanted downward toward the apex) or positive (slanted away from the apex toward the outside of the turn). In addition, there are turns that have an increasing radius while others have a decreasing radius. All of these factors impact one's speed through the turn.

When entering a corner and finding that we have too much speed, one option is to turn the wheel slightly and then turn it back. Doing this will slow the car down (known in racing as *scrubbing speed off*). This is better than touching the brake, since doing that will shift weight to the nose of the car.

Another tactic is to *avoid going to too low a gear* in the corner, since doing so can cause more deceleration than desired. Being in a higher gear makes it possible to carry more speed through the corner and enables better modulation of the throttle upon exit. Being a gear too low could put the motor too high on the torque curve. And if you don't have just the right throttle pedal, the result could be removing weight from the nose when turning, which will make it more difficult to turn. This leads to another trick—shifting in the middle of the corner. This is useful if you find you have overslowed the entry or if you are going too fast. Upshifting while taking the corner makes it easier to get to throttle. These tricks of the trade, when deployed at the right times, can lead to better performance on the track.

Our next area of focus is *braking*. Once you reach maximum speed, the objective is to maintain it for as long as possible. This means you want to begin your braking as late as possible without sacrificing the turn-in. We use markers to identify when we should brake. These markers are usually at the end of the straights, starting at 400 feet and going down to 100 feet. But they can begin at 600 feet, depending on the track and relative speeds.

In *braking and cornering*, we aim to maintain a balance between the front and rear of the car. When we are driving and braking at the limit of grip, if the weight is not spread evenly, the tires become overloaded and can cause you to lose grip. It's akin to asking for more than 100 percent of something—you're not going to get it. If you are braking at a threshold of 80 percent, then you can only add 20 percent of steering angle before the grip of the tire vanishes. So maximum braking is typically done in a straight line before asking for any steering wheel input. This also applies to throttle and steering off the corner.

With *threshold braking*, you exert maximum brake pressure at the initial hit of the brake. Then, as the car decelerates, you trail off until you have totally released the brake at the apex of the corner. Most GT (Grand Touring) racecars do not have power brakes, but today's streetcars all have power brakes. The power brake booster multiplies the pressure you put on the pedal, generally by a factor of four. So in a streetcar you only need to put four hundred pounds of pressure on the pedal to get sixteen hundred pounds of pressure in the hydraulic brake system. In racing, the absence of power brakes allows us to better modulate or control the brake's release. We modulate because we are managing the deceleration and therefore the amount of weight we are removing from the front wheels (we need some weight on the outside front tire because we want the car to turn). Therefore, if drivers want sixteen hundred pounds of pressure in the system, our right leg needs to put it there.

Another part of driving and braking is reaction time. A normal person takes about 1.5–2 seconds to move their foot from the throttle to the brake. A typical racecar driver will take about 0.5 seconds. At high speeds, the 1.0–1.5 second differential is a lot of track space. Realistically, if you are following a racecar driver and he brakes quickly, you are likely to rear-end him because your reaction time is not as fast.

This raises another subject—*physical fitness*. Professional racing drivers are some of the most physically fit athletes in the world. Their type of fitness will depend on the type of car they drive and the series in which they participate. Generally, endurance drivers, of which I am one, train to have a stronger but leaner body mass that can endure prolonged exercise, heat, and g-forces throughout a racing stint, which can be an hour or more. Then we can rest—but we may need to drive again in the same race (see appendixes A and B).

To *make a pass*, we can use the opportunity of corner entry. We can attempt to brake in a shorter distance than our competitors, which we say is to "outbrake" them. Some drivers are very good at late braking ("late brakers"), so we need to consider our competitors when using this technique. It will depend on where you are longitudinally on the track relative to the corner you are approaching. If it is a right-hand corner and you are inside the car being passed, you will need to brake sooner than they will. Why? Because you will need to slow down enough to make the corner without hitting the other driver when he turns into the corner (otherwise you might go straight and slide off the track). The timing and concentration for orchestrating "outbraking" passes is critical to success.

Professional drivers generally have similar but varied driving techniques. We all know what to do, but how we do those things varies. For example, some drivers adapt better to select types of tracks and select turns within those tracks. There are complex turns that can be slower and have complex or changing radii, and there are higher-speed turns where the driver needs to comprehend the speed of the corner. High-speed corners can be mentally challenging, at least at first—there is a big difference between going through a turn at 80 mph versus 120 mph. A driver's ability to adapt to the type of turn can influence his speed in select corners or tracks and how competitors can exploit these differences.

Many of the GT cars used in endurance racing (and single-seat cars like IndyCars) have *front and rear down force or aerodynamics.* This is achieved through wings and dive planes on the front and rear of the car as well as the design of the car's under tray. These devices are designed in a wind tunnel by aerodynamicists. The air passing over the top and bottom of the car creates downward force on the body. Faster moving air has a lower pressure than slower moving air. Therefore, managing the air speed differential over and under the car can contribute to down force in select areas of the track. Improved down force can increase the speeds a driver is able to carry through the corner, which will drive lap times down. Generally, more down force will have a decreasing effect on top speed because of the aero drag the wings create. The more down force that is created, the greater the corner speeds and the greater the g-force on the driver and the car. One g-force equals the weight of your body. Two Gs is twice your body weight.

Drivers must also be able to withstand accidents and impacts. The increase in dissipated energy from a sudden stop at 130 mph versus 100 mph is not just a 30 percent increase. Rather, the increase in energy is a function of the square of the velocity. Therefore, it is a 69 percent increase:

$$(130 \times 130) / (100 \times 100) = 16{,}900/10{,}000$$

The attendant effects are mediated by the driver's level of physical fitness as well as the type and level of that fitness. Upper body, core, and leg strength are all impacted. Whether the car has power steering in combination with the type and level of aerodynamics affects the type and level of requisite fitness. Finally, the length and type of races (endurance versus sprint races) also play a role in the fitness profile of a driver.

Let's get back to the racing game. Once through the corner, we begin the process of *applying power* to get back up to speed, but we do so somewhat gradually. We call this *power application modulation*. We don't just go to full power—we go to some degree of partial power and then to full power. We modulate or manage the power application depending on whether the car is fully turned. If it's not, then we need to be sure we do not use too much power, as doing so will remove weight from the front tires at a point when we want the car to turn. It could also overpower the rear tires and cause a spin.

Over time, racing has become increasingly complex because of the *data and engineering* being introduced. Today's racecars generate reams of data; we can generate as much data as we want, thanks to the availability of monitoring sensors and computers. There are sensors for throttle position, brake position, and steering angle, plus in-car video that enables one to see hand position, track position, traffic, etc. All of these data and videos can be viewed side by side in comparison to one's teammates or co-drivers. This leads to the evolution of capabilities across all drivers.

These data points are analyzed by race engineers in an effort to understand the driver's critique of the car and what adjustments to the car (air pressure, sway bars, shock settings, spring rates, etc.) might be needed based on track and weather conditions. Once a change is identified, that change is made and a driver verifies whether the change has been positive, negative, or neutral. That change might be corroborated with another driver, particularly if the team is considering making the same change on a sister car of a multi-car team. This process of change, verification, and corroboration should fine-tune a car to a track. The environmental conditions play a role in this analysis: track temperature, time of day, precipitation, and ambient temperature are all factors that could result in changes on or to the car at a given track on a given day.

Then there are the *team members and mechanics*. Teams usually have one or two race haulers (tractor trailer trucks) that carry the cars and spare parts. These haulers are typically parked in some systematic fashion in a paddock. The hauler often has a lounge where the drivers and potentially engineers review data and videos. Generally, the engineers attempt to diagnose car characteristics, while the drivers review data and videos in an effort to improve lap times. The mechanics are usually outside the hauler working on the cars, often under a huge awning that protects them from the sun and rain. The mechanics are the most important part of the team, particularly the "over-the-wall" guys who refuel the car and change tires quickly during pit stops. The drivers literally place their lives in the hands of these team members. (Nothing good happens when a front wheel comes off at 170 mph.) These folks make every effort to inspect parts and replace them before a failure occurs.

On the racecourse, *flag marshals* communicate with the drivers via a series of colored flags. Flags can be simply informational—to indicate that a slower car or safety vehicle is ahead (white flag) or that a faster car is approaching from behind (a blue flag with a yellow diagonal stripe). Other flags offer more important information, such as a standing yellow flag, which indicates a car ahead has spun out but off-track, as opposed to a waving yellow, which generally means the car that spun out is on the racing surface. There is also a debris flag (yellow with red stripes), indicating that there is an on-track object or slippery condition.

RACING ROOM

In racing there are rules of the road, though nearly all of them are unwritten. One rule is to stay in your space. All cars on the track are allowed "racing room" or space. This does not mean that another car needs to give way or concede to another competitor—that wouldn't be racing, would it? I can go side-by-side with some competitors around a turn without us touching. These are good clean competitors. But there are those who you can't trust. These will punt you off-track.

The lines on the track

One of my fellow driving instructors once asked a group of students what the lines on the track mean. There were a wide variety of responses. The answer: absolutely nothing. They are merely guides for us—the edge of the track, center of the track, where the curbing begins and ends, etc. At select tracks, there are things known as *track limits*, which generally apply to the exits of select turns—they want you to keep at least two wheels (left or right side) on some of the curbing (remember that shortening the radius of the turn on the inside leads to higher corner speed and can lead to going off-track on the exit). This is generally to control competition and defines the racing surface.

RESPECT

The "racing room" material above means having respect for one another while on track. We are all competitors and we all want to win. We need to be as aggressive as possible, but we should be respectful. There are many good drivers out there who can balance aggression and respect—but there are many who can't, and you need to find out who they are and proceed with caution.

HAND POSITION

If you observe racecar drivers, you will notice that they always have both hands on the steering wheel and they are generally located at the nine-o'clock and three-o'clock positions. Having both hands on the wheel allows you to quickly turn or maneuver in the event something happens in front or alongside of you. I have translated this to the everyday road as well. One friend who has driven with me on long trips once said that he had never seen me without both hands on the wheel, even when I'm driving my truck or towing. It simply stabilizes your steering application and allows for a quick response.

SUMMARY

The prime objective in driving a racecar is to lower one's lap time. This is generally viewed as the fastest average speed the car can achieve on a given day at a given track. All the information or factors covered above contribute to achieving such a lap time. We do this in the quest to be faster than the other cars in our classification.

This overview of racing and the general environment in which we operate will help you understand the material that follows, as I connect my racing experiences to everyday life.

2

Three Things You Need in Order to Do Anything

"Attitude is a choice. Happiness is a choice. Optimism is a choice. Kindness is a choice. Giving is a choice. Respect is a choice. Whatever choice you make makes you. Choose wisely."

Roy T. Bennett

Three things are needed to accomplish anything: proper tools, know-how, and time. If you are missing any of the three, the project cannot be completed.

PROPER TOOLS

When I started racing in 1991, I had a 1976 BMW 2002, which I had purchased from a driving instructor at the first SCCA school I attended. The seller ran an auto repair business and agreed to help me along in those first years. But I didn't know much about repairing or working on a BMW.

One of the first tasks was adjusting the valves. The guy got me started (take valve cover off, etc.) and then told me to take a 10mm wrench and have at it. After about twenty minutes of pure frustration, I sheepishly went to him and said that I needed some help. It was not going well. He came down to where I was working and said, "Show me what you're doing." I did. He said I was lacking "the special tool." I said I didn't think I had received the memo about a "special tool" to adjust the 2002's valves.

The tool was to hold an eccentric while tightening the rocker arm. The eccentric, in turn, takes lash out of the valve. You use this eccentric to provide the right amount of gap. It looked like part of a coat hanger, about six inches long with a bend on each end going in opposite directions. It was the kind of thing you could make *if* you knew what it looked like—or even knew you needed it.

The point is that because I didn't have that tool—heck, I didn't know there was one—I could not get started. This small piece of wire was *the* big hang up. Without it, I couldn't go any further than "go."

What does this have to do with life? A lot. If you are beginning any project, you first need to assess whether there are any special tools or knowledge that may be required in order to complete it. It is best to assess the situation in the beginning and then assemble all of the required tools. This will help ensure that those tools are available when needed, regardless of the sequence in which those needs might occur. Without the right tools, you can't get started doing anything.

KNOW-HOW

I had been racing for only a short time when my car got in an accident. I had a teammate in the automobile repair business who told me he would help me with the repairs, but I would need to do some of the work myself at his shop, leaving the more difficult tasks to him. I agreed. We reached a point where we needed to remove the front bumper from the car. He instructed me to take several wrenches and remove the bumper bolts, which I did, and then I was to work on a part called the nose panel. Once I had removed the bumper, the front bumper brackets became a problem. I worked and worked on those brackets, but I couldn't get them off. Finally, I went to him and told him I was having a problem. He came down to where I was working and said, "Show me what you're doing." Once I did so, he told me, "You need to take these bolts off in the following order," which he then specified. Once I did that the brackets came right off.

TIME

Time is critical to fulfilling the needs of any project, task, or venture. Even if one has the proper tools and know-how, not having enough time means the job cannot get done. Time needs to be part of the planning for any project, job, trip, etc. Failing to include consideration of the time needed will undoubtedly lead to failure, or—if you are lucky—suboptimal results at a minimum.

How does this carry back over into racing? Tools are a critical part of maintaining a car, both before you get to the track and while you are there. It is important to have all the tools that you could reasonably expect to need. In addition, the know-how is important in case you don't have someone with you at the track who knows what to do. And, of course, there's always limited time. Tools and know-how are usually the Achilles' heels with

21

any track-based project. An ancillary benefit of having tools and know-how is that you usually need less time than would otherwise be necessary. Put differently, if you have the tools, be sure you know how to use them.

So keep tools, know-how, and time in mind as you plan for any project, in all aspects of your life.

3

Three Steps That Are Needed to Achieve Anything

"Far and away the best prize that life has to offer is the chance to work hard at work worth doing."

Theodore Roosevelt

Three things must be in place in order to successfully implement anything: an idea, the ability to develop that idea into something that can be implemented, and execution. If any of these three elements are missing or inadequate, the given product, service, or concept will surely fail. Let's discuss each of these elements and then relate them to one another.

Much of what I've written here originally came from a man named Mike Vance, who worked for the Disney Company and was fortunate enough to work directly with Walt Disney. I first heard many of these concepts around 1980, so they are not new—they simply work. Much of my thinking about work, about racing, and about everyday life came as a byproduct of listening to Mike's speeches.

THE IDEA

An idea is needed to facilitate achieving anything. This can be an engineering idea or an idea for a product or service. These ideas or concepts usually come from a basic knowledge of the area or business and usually represent an innovation of some kind. It can even be an adaptation of a previous product or service. Thus, new products can remake an old product. It can also adapt that old product for a new use. An example was my idea to launch a race team in 2006. I had been in and around the racing world for fifteen years, so I had a general understanding of race teams and I saw the need for a team that could help me meet my objectives.

ABILITY TO DEVELOP THE IDEA

Next, the idea needs to be developed into something that can be implemented or used for some purpose. This might be engineering based in certain circumstances, but it can also require other skills. In my prior profession as a consultant, I would have an idea for a new service and develop it for hospitals. Then we would work out a plan to market that service to the hospitals that needed it. This took the form of identifying potential clients in advance, as the service often applied only to select hospitals. So we developed the product, identified who needed it, and then marketed it to that select group.

For my race team, while I thought I had a good idea, I also knew I would need help executing it, so I hired someone. He helped find the necessary talent—everything from drivers to mechanics to public relations experts. Implementing new ideas can—and usually does—require engineering assistance. We might have an idea about how to change the set up on the car, then work with the manufacturer to develop a way to implement it.

EXECUTE

This is a critical element in the process. You must be able to execute the plan or product (and do it well) in order to accomplish your objective. This requires both the correct approach and the right people. And execution is a never-ending process that's rarely (if ever) perfected. Some members of my race team, for example, wear GoPro devices on our helmets, and we are always analyzing the footage to see how we can improve. We are always focusing on our starts, as well as the overall race strategy. We need to get the start right, get on throttle at the same time the leader does, be in the right gear, and have our tires and brakes warmed up. Everything needs to be ready to go because we can't be guessing about what to do when we get to the first turn.

SUMMARY

A poor idea is not going to get you anywhere. Therefore, it's critical to figure out whether the idea is sound at the very beginning. Explore the idea from as many perspectives as possible. Next, there needs to be a critical assessment of what is needed to develop that idea. Is the talent available internally or does it need to be procured? Are new hires needed to get the talent? Once the talent issue has been settled, there needs to be a process for developing the idea.

As the idea is developed, you need to continually test it to assure it's still on the right track for its intended use. Once you have a good idea that's properly developed, you need to execute.

A great football play that's developed well but poorly executed is not going to put any points on the scoreboard. Execution cannot be downplayed. You need to have the right folks doing the implementing. They need to understand the idea and the plan and execute well. We have seen too many poorly executed ideas that lead to failures in business and life.

An idea, the ability to develop that idea into something that can be implemented, and proper execution. You need all three. Without any one of them, the final product will be suboptimal— and may not result in anything at all.

4

Principle-Based Actions: Having Good Guiding Principles

"You cannot change the circumstances but you can change yourself. That is something you have charge of."

Jim Rohn

The Golden Rule—do unto others as you would have others do unto you—not only applies in everyday life, but in racing too. You also need to be true to yourself. Think, reflect, be patient. As we say, "What goes around comes around."

As racers we all want all the track time we can get. However, in certain situations we need to step back and accept that we can't always get every second. (Racers are very competitive individuals and routinely push the envelope.)

In 2021, my team was racing at Sebring International Raceway in the Ferrari Challenge series. Someone from another team had a crash that damaged his car beyond repair. Later in the day I saw the driver at the awards ceremony for one of my teammates, who had finished third in his race. I asked the driver if he was okay. The driver responded that he was fine but mentioned that the crash was caused by a brake failure going into Turn 13. He said he had noticed the day before that the brakes felt funny, but he didn't bother to say anything.

I politely responded—scolding—that whenever any driver feels something unusual, they need to tell their crew so they can find out what's wrong before going back on track. I said that drivers can hurt themselves, as well as anyone else on track with them. Indeed, that type of failure can be catastrophic even under the best circumstances, given that the cars are traveling as fast as 180 mph.

I told him that the day before in practice I had left pit lane and by the time I got to Turn 5 I radioed my crew and said the brakes did not feel right. They told me to be safe and return to pit lane. They checked the brakes out and determined that they should try to bleed them right there. (To bleed the brakes requires pumping the brake pedal and holding it, and then opening a valve on the brake caliper that allows some brake fluid to escape along with any trapped air in the brake line, thus preventing the brake from fading or failing.) Once they finished, I tested the brakes in the safest spots I could find without any other cars around.

The moral of the story is—to paraphrase the TSA—if you feel something, you need to say something. This is particularly true when safety is involved—yours or others'.

This applies to life, too. Whether it's a safety situation or something else, when something is awry you must say something. This is a fairness issue, and it relates back to the Golden Rule. Things you do or see can affect others in a negative way. I'm not suggesting one should be a vigilante, but when something is inherently wrong, we should not behave in a manner that exacerbates the issue or situation. And as much as possible, we should not allow others to do so either. If we all play our collective parts, things will get better for all of us.

5

Always Looking and Thinking Ahead

"It is not the strongest of the species that survives, not the
most intelligent, but the one most responsive to change."
Charles Darwin

In racing and life, we must always plan ahead. These plans can
change—and likely will. But they are reference points for us to
pursue. Changes in the environment can be positive or negative.
Either way we must respond in a sensible, thoughtful manner.

STRATEGY

We are always thinking ahead in racing. This applies to race
strategy and to what a driver does when the race starts. Thinking
ahead allows us to have options. As other factors change, this can

change as well, but it always pays to look ahead because the time horizon is moving toward us so quickly. We start with a general strategy that we believe is right for the track and what we want to accomplish. However, that plan may change slightly—or a lot. It depends on how things evolve.

With race strategy, we are looking at the total environment, which includes what everyone else is doing. We need to know our fuel mileage, of course, but also the fuel mileage of our competitors, since that determines when they need to refuel. In endurance racing, pit stops are critical. The team who makes the fewest and shortest stops will be in a better position to win.

In endurance racing, the race is at least as much about strategy and fuel mileage as it is about driving. The team monitors our car's fuel burn as well as that of our competitors, when they make a pit stop, whether it's a full stop (tire, fuel, and driver change) or just a fuel top off, how many seconds of fuel they took, etc. All contribute to whether we can or should make another stop, or whether we can make do with the fuel we have. There are folks dedicated to this function and they sit on a timing stand, which is referred to as a "pit box." The pit box has electronics that help them see the lap times and progress of all competitors, including closed-circuit television coverage of all the parts of the track.

DRIVING

Driving racecars at speed requires attention, focus, and looking ahead. This was emphasized to me when traveling with a friend. He was worried about cleaning the windshield at every stop for fuel. It occurred to me that I really did not notice the bugs and debris on my car's windshield because my focal point was not the windshield (as it was my friend's). My focal point was 600–800 feet in front of us.

Driving racecars at 150 mph requires this longer focal point. If I'm going 150 mph and something occurs 200 feet away and directly in front of the car, I simply cannot react that quickly. Normal people take about 1.5–2.0 seconds to get their right foot off the accelerator and onto the brake. For a race driver this reaction takes about half a second—or 3–4 times faster. But even for us, we simply cannot react quickly enough to avert something 200 feet in front of us at 150 mph.

For a race start, I always have a plan. This plan is a series of strategies based on the environment and the cars around me. Some of what I take into consideration includes where I am on the grid (inside/outside); who is in front and behind me for several rows of cars; their relative lap times, where they are in the standings (which can dictate how aggressive they might be or need to be on the start); what other cars in other classes are near me that I might need to deal with; and the experience of the drivers in the surrounding cars. It's a very complex set of factors. What's important here is the old racing adage "in order to finish first, we must first finish."

Many competitors feel that since the cars are in such close proximity at the start, they can move ahead of others during the race. The result is that they are often overly aggressive. Endurance racing is a thinking game, not a "go-fast" game. We often need to conserve fuel and let our competitors get ahead for a while if we believe they are going to need to make more stops than we are.

Calculating this depends on the cars, their fuel capacity, and their fuel burn. The harder we run, the more fuel we burn. This is monitored as part of the strategy. We have been in situations where we have let the other cars go ahead of us and then just maintained the gap. Once we were certain we were not going to need to make any more fuel stops, we chased them down. In one particular situation, there were three cars ahead us and they all ran out of fuel two turns from the end of the race. We passed them all and won—all because we had developed a strategy around this situation. The start is a place where the race can be lost, but never won.

In endurance racing, the starting driver needs to hand the car over to the second driver (who is usually the faster of the pair) in a strong enough position for that individual to finish the race in as high a position as the car is capable of.

MORAL

This is a lot like life. Once we develop our plan, we need to see what data are out there, collect and evaluate that data, develop our strategy, evaluate our strategy as it rolls out and as conditions change, then determine whether our initial strategy was correct—as well as what needs to be changed and when—and then change the strategy as appropriate and decide on timing.

This is what you need to anticipate for essentially every project or endeavor in life. Assume there will be changes to the situation and that plans will shift. This speaks to the importance of thinking and looking as far ahead as possible. It's also important to create lead time to be able to thoughtfully react to whatever has occurred and to secure additional information or data in order to make the revised plan.

Mike Vance, who I talked about in Chapter 3, released a collection of CDs several years ago under the title, "Creative Leadership System." On one of the CDs, he recounted a time when

Walt Disney was attending a cocktail reception with many of the other animated motion picture studios, such as Walter Lantz Productions, which produced Woody Woodpecker. They asked Walt what he was working on and he told them. After a while, Walt's staff pulled him aside and said, "Walt, you are telling them exactly what we are doing. Aren't you afraid they will steal it?" Walt responded, *"It doesn't matter. I can create faster than they can steal."*

This idea has always stuck with me. It is a very positive and forward-looking philosophy. I have recounted many things in the preceding text that speak to looking forward and being positive. I have found that by focusing forward you will virtually always be ahead of whatever is back there.

In sum, thinking ahead and looking as far ahead as possible greatly increases your potential for success.

6

Ocular Driving: We Drive Where We Look

"A goal is not always meant to be reached; it often serves simply as something to aim at."

Bruce Lee

A good rule of thumb to guide us in everyday life is to always focus forward. Why? Because that's where we're going. That's why the windshield in a car is bigger than the mirrors and rear window. It's not surprising that we drive where we look. This is the mantra in racing.

On the racetrack, we tell students to look where they want the car to go. Once you have focused on where you want to go, your body's response is for your hands and feet to locomote to effectuate that path. Your body has been in situations where your arms reflexively turn in the direction you are looking. Once your eyes pick up and focus on the apex of a corner, your arms will turn in that direction. It becomes a subconscious reflexive action. In racing we are trained to do this or we adapt to it over time. Then we look through the corner toward the exit. Doing so allows us to navigate through the corner faster.

Have you ever had something suddenly catch your attention on the sidewalk? Think about how you turned toward what caught your attention. That's exactly my point.

I had a neighbor who ran into a tree. She said the tree jumped out in front of her. What happened was that she had purchased three potted plants and had them in the passenger footwell of her car. A bump jostled the plants and one of them fell over toward the outside of the car. She instinctively leaned over to sit the plant upright again. As she did, she held onto the steering wheel, so as she leaned the car turned to the right—which was where the tree was on the side of the road. We always kidded her because she said the tree jumped out in front of her. What else could she say?

When we look where we are going, we tend to go in that direction. This is related to focus. Once we have an idea of where we want to go, we can get there by ocular driving and keeping our sights on that goal. Many of us fail to accomplish a goal because we either lose focus or fail to keep our eyes on that goal—ocular driving.

Concentration is key here. We can lose our concentration if we have too many distractions. It's like looking out the car window and seeing all the things on the side of the road. Later in the book, I describe driving at night. It might be better in some ways to drive at night. During the day, our peripheral vision picks up a lot of things: trees, landmarks, signs, people, etc. At night, we generally can't see those things because our headlights only illuminate a certain field of vision. At night, we tend to concentrate on what's in front of us.

If you focus on where you want to go and use the concept of ocular driving to stay focused, you will generally have a better outcome even if you don't reach your specific goal. In the end, you'll be farther ahead than you otherwise would be. Try it.

7

Passing: Under Braking, on the Straight, and in the Corner

"The only man who never makes mistakes is the man who never does anything."

Theodore Roosevelt

Driving racecars fast is one thing; racing is quite another. Racing and race craft require different skillsets and levels of aggressiveness. In racing, the point is to beat the other driver in the same class. There is a sense of fairness in the competition, as there are rules ("the letter of the law") and rules of etiquette ("the spirit of the law").

As I mentioned earlier, driving fast is fundamentally about corner speed, and corner speed is facilitated by better or faster corner entry, which means better braking into the corner. Faster corner speeds mean we can get back to throttle sooner, which influences our speed down the following straightaway. The end result is faster lap times. However, the exact exercise of these principles changes when we are racing, as we may need to sacrifice something to get past another competitor.

There are several ways to pass:

UNDER BRAKING

There are aerodynamic effects related to each racecar. A car's aero generally allows it to go through the corner faster. However, on the straights these aero modifications slow the car down. It's much like when you put your hand out the car window. If its side is facing toward the front, it has better aero effect. But when you turn it with the palm facing forward, the result is aero drag.

This aero drag slows the car because the motor cannot overpower it. The faster the car is traveling, the greater the aero drag effect. However, if drafting behind a car, the removal of the aero drag can theoretically add horsepower and speed to our car. That's because the car in front is making a hole in the air for us, which makes it easier to pass.

A few years ago, I was racing at Indianapolis on the track that's home to the Indy 500 and trailing another competitor. It was clear to my co-driver that the car in front was holding me up. I was faster in many places but couldn't pass. We concluded that the best place to try to make a pass was the end of the front straight, which was a very long run down to a very tight right-hand corner. The driver of the car I was following was what we call a "late braker," which is someone who brakes very late and hard. (I am a very late braker, too.) This meant that I needed to be just behind that car when we entered the front straight in order to maximize the draft.

I followed that car onto the front straight but I was still about a car length behind. I kept getting closer and finally got right on his bumper. My co-driver was counseling me on the radio to "stay in the draft, stay in the draft." Then, at the last moment, he said, "go for it." I pulled out and went for the pass. Side by side, we both broke very late, but I was on the inside and finally had the nose of my car in front of the other driver. The complicating factor was that there were two of us late brakers trying to get into the same tight corner first. I succeeded in making the pass and staying ahead, so the other car followed me for a few corners. After about a lap, I couldn't see the car behind me. I managed to clear a few other cars that I had caught in front of me. We finished well.

The moral here is that you need to clearly understand your circumstances. Another opinion can help here. The front car holding me up indicated that I needed to get past in order to move ahead. Then, in making that pass, it was important to know where we both were and how far I had moved up. It is not always necessary to lead. There is nothing wrong with following unless those in front of you are preventing you from moving up. A key question is when to make the move and whether you have enough time to reach the end goal once you do. All of this is impacted by the relative speeds of your car and the cars ahead of you.

This too can resemble life, since the ability to do quality work on a project or to meet one's goals is often determined by timing. There can be situations where it might be strategically better to stay behind and save fuel, such as in endurance races where the cars further ahead might run out.

ON THE STRAIGHT

Another similar scenario is getting close to the car ahead prior to the straight. If we are very close, using the draft is an option, as it will make it possible to pull out and get alongside the other car earlier in the straight. In these scenarios, we can get alongside the competitor and potentially pull away. However, if the straight is long enough, the other car may be able to get back behind us and pass us again on the same straight—or use an outbraking maneuver as mentioned before. The timing depends on the length of the straight, how much draft we can get, and the timing of the attempted pass.

All of this underscores the importance of timing. We still need to have data, such as the speed of the other cars, our position in the race, and the magnitude of the gap between us and those ahead of us. But the timing of the move is critical.

CORNER ENTRY PASSES

In these situations, we are always analyzing where we are better than our competitors. Is it at corner entry, in the corner, or on the straight? If our car is better on corner entry and in the corner, then the best option may be to attempt a pass in the corner. If we can outbrake them, then the best option is corner entry. But if we are better in the corner, then perhaps we can go around the outside while going through the corner and make the pass. If we are better on the corner exit, maybe we can get very close in the corner and lay on the power sooner than they do. It all depends on the relative strengths of the cars and the drivers.

We usually make these judgments when we are on the track. We are looking for where the car ahead is better than we are and vice versa. Once we know these things, we can develop a strategy to plan our pass or overtake.

This is much like life or business. We can assess the environment to gauge the situation. We use relative strengths to develop approaches to leverage these strengths and weaknesses and match our strengths to our competitors' weaknesses. To properly do this, we need to take a clear look at our own performance and the performance of our competitors—and do so without biases. Clarity of perspective, understanding, and thinking is required. Third parties can add perspective in these situations. These perspectives can come from those directly involved, but also from those outside the situation. The insights that emerge can be factored into our decision-making, which will influence whether or not we succeed.

8

When the Green Flag Drops, the Bullshit Stops

"Half the world is composed of people who have something to say and can't, and the other half who have nothing to say and keep on saying it."

Robert Frost

The great thing about racing is that you cannot dispute things. There's a track of a defined distance; a stopwatch or timing equipment; and someone to watch. You either go fast or you don't. That's it.

In many areas of life, we come up with ways to explain away our performance, or the results of a project, or anything else. Much of that can be bullshit, just folks talking. Talk is a lot cheaper than performance.

There are many egos in sports, and racing is no different. It is ego that underpins the greatness of many athletes. Their egos drive them to higher and higher levels of performance. However, with this pursuit of high performance comes a great desire to perform. This performance often drives continued employment or higher pay or both. The greater the degree of competition for slots for athletes, the greater the degree of competition generally. This is where egos can and do come into play—and often in a big way. In racing, there is competition for seats in cars and sponsorship monies for a team or driver. As the number of seats contracts, the intensity of the competition grows.

These egos lead to a lot of talk about the greatness of drivers. We need to believe we are great in order to portray ourselves as great. This may or may not be the case in reality. In fact, we as drivers are participating in a sport; whether we want to acknowledge it or not, there is a hierarchy.

While drivers' performances vary, they can be affected by the type of track—some have lots of turns, for example, while others have more straightaways. Tighter turns may be more technical, and some drivers and cars are better suited to those. Weather can also affect performance, with rain being the most common factor. Thus, performance is relative, but we are all in some way egocentric.

There are constants that allow performance to be gauged on any given day. The track, for example, has a fixed configuration and length. Similarly, the timing system provides relative lap times, while the scoring tells us how we're faring relative to our competitors. We even have a predicted lap time on the dash of the car so we know how we are doing. Another constant is the sanctioning body that attempts to regulate the playing field and keep it as level as possible with measures like restricting power, adding weight, and prescribing ride height.

In racing, we say that when the green flag drops—marking the start of the race—the bullshit stops. This is the moment when, regardless of our egos and talk, we need to put up or shut up.

The scenario I've just described has some parallels to everyday life. We encounter big egos and they can affect us in ways big or small. Many folks talk a great game. Perhaps that's their ego talking, or perhaps they need to try to portray a high image. Maybe they need it for their own internal or interpersonal reasons. Or perhaps they need to feel superior to those of us outside their circle. Whatever the reason, as they do this it affects others around them.

When I encounter these types of folks, I usually have one of two reactions. One is to ignore them and their egocentric behaviors. I may not need them or I may not really want to understand or engage with them. In these situations, I usually attempt to transition to another subject. My other reaction is to engage with these individuals because I want to work with them on some level. However, I need to be subtle in informing or suggesting to them that they might not be as well informed as they think they are. I do this to get them to a point where we can work together. If collaborators in a project are too egocentric, then there is a question about whether they can work together and how.

There are many times when I encounter these egocentric folks. The best course of action is not to engage with them. But first, we need to determine whether and if we *need* to work with them—or how much we need them, whether they can be replaced, and if we can deal with them. If the determination is made to work with them, it will inform how we move forward. It may be necessary to soften them up a bit by letting them know they are not as smart as they thought. The goal should be to get them to the point where they stop the bullshit.

9

Racing in the Rain:
It Gets Complicated

"Racing in the rain is like cooking bacon in the nude, somewhere along the line you are going to get burnt."

Bill Riddle

Racing is a complex undertaking even in ideal weather conditions. However, when it rains—or is merely wet—the com-
plexity quotient goes up a few notches. Generally, racecars are set
up to race in dry conditions. As such, they have a stiffer suspension, which is related to the track and the conditions on the given
day. However, the rain suggests that we soften the suspension
(and perhaps the shock settings), maybe even re-valve the shocks
if the rules permit, soften the front and/or rear sway bars, and
maybe even change the spring rates. In less-than-ideal condi-

tions, you want the suspension to be as compliant as possible. With a softer suspension, the tire contact patches will be more flexible and will more closely follow the undulations of the racing surface. This is a good thing. Also, rain tires are a little narrower than dry tires and a little softer. The difference in width allows the tire to track better in the water.

Racing in the rain can be good or bad depending on the car's setup. When the setup is good, racing in the rain is not too bad. But a poor setup translates to a lot of slipping and sliding. When a track is wet, lap times are always slower than when the track is dry, and the differential varies depending on the length of the track. Because of this, there are several variables to consider when making decisions in wet conditions—and even good decisions can be upended by mistakes made by other racers.

Rain tires (like regular tires) have deep grooves that allow the water to track out. This prevents hydroplaning, when the car loses stability because the tire is not fully in contact with the track or road surface. The narrowness of rain tires allows them to track through the water better. Rain tires are softer too, which makes it problematic to run them on a dry track; they get hot because the soft rubber needs water to cool the tread, and if the tread gets hot the rubber will chunk off and grip will decrease dramatically. Dry tires by comparison do not have tread. As such, they work very well in on a dry track because you have more tire surface in contact with the track or road (the contact patch). Conversely, dry tires do not allow water to channel out from beneath, which makes their grip very uncertain. Driving on a wet track with dry tires can be a treacherous, nerve-wracking situation.

In the wet, we must adapt and change our driving approach. The normal line around a dry track is down by the curbs, but that's not so in the wet.

There are two reasons to change our line and approach in the wet. First, all of the water that hits the track drains to its lowest level, which can lead this water to accumulate and pool at the bottom of the track, down by the apex. In the wet it's better to be at least a half-car off the downside edge of the track. Second, most cars run by the apex in the dry, which is at least 95 percent of the time. Therefore, the stones in the blacktop down by the apex get polished and their grip is less than the grip up high. So another important issue is how high we should run on a given track on a given day. The only way to find out is through experimentation.

Another trick to driving in the rain is being in a higher gear than normal. That's because the car is not in as powerful a torque position, which can make it tail sensitive. Also, to mitigate the effects of all the water on the track, we can choose to drive in the tracks of the car in front of us. Once the car in front goes through the water on the track, the tires will evacuate the water under the tire. Those tracks have much less water on them. When the trailing car drives in those tracks it can have better grip, which means it will be slightly faster than the car going through the full wet conditions. This approach can be used on public roads too.

Another complicating factor in the rain could be the specific track we are racing on. Many tracks are long (over four miles) or shaped so that the legs are longer. This sets up a scenario in which it could be raining on one area of the track and dry on another. This means we need to be strategic or selective in choosing our tires, as rain tires do not work well in the dry and vice versa.

ROAD AMERICA

One time we were racing at Road America during a torrential rainstorm. The rain had been nonstop for about twenty-four hours. Water was everywhere. When it gets this bad, the grass off the side of the track gets so saturated that it can't absorb any additional water. With nowhere for the water on the track to go, it stays there and accumulates, resulting in big puddles.

We had three practice sessions scheduled during the rainstorm. We skipped all of them. In looking at the weather forecast, the rain looked to be passing through, and the following few days were going to be dry and sunny. While giving up track time generally winds up being a disadvantage, track time in the wet only makes you more prepared for the race *if* you're going to race in the wet. Practicing in the wet does nothing for you or the car if you will be racing in the dry, since the conditions are so dramatically different. Plus there is more risk.

This late-afternoon session had tons of water on the track and puddles everywhere. About half the field—roughly twenty cars—stayed in the paddock with us. We were totally bored and wondering if we should have gone out. Of the cars that went out, about half crashed. To make matters worse, about half of those that crashed could not be repaired and had to sit out the race and thus scored no points.

This scenario has parallels to the decisions we make in everyday life. When evaluating what to do, we seem to get ourselves into positions where we think we need to decide or take action. We push ourselves into believing that we must act and do something. By doing so, we can overlook the consideration of the risks associated with making the decision. Choosing to do nothing might be the right decision. We need to implicitly make a risk-reward comparison. Is the risk of any decision or action worth the reward? Many of us fail to recognize that there are risks or consequences (some known and some unknown) related to every decision we make. We need to gather as much information as we can before making the final decision. We need to ask ourselves several questions: Is there risk? What are those risks? And are those risks worth the potential rewards?

VIRGINIA INTERNATIONAL RACEWAY

Another time, we were racing at Virginia International Raceway (VIR) and it had rained the day before. The track was a mix of wet, damp, and drying. The weather forecast indicated it would be dry for the race, but it definitely wasn't dry. Conditions were not ideal. The sun was out, but the track was still damp and the degree of dampness varied based on where you were on the track. I was on the track and needed the practice. I was looking forward to the race the following day because it would help determine whether I would win the International GT Championship. There is a portion of the track known as the "uphill S's." One way to build a fast lap time at VIR is to be able to take the "uphill" flat out, at full throttle.

When it came time to qualify, things were uneventful until about halfway through the session. The conditions were still damp, so I was not flat out. But I wanted a fast time. There was a car about ten car lengths behind me and we were driving the lap at the same pace. I knew he was a good driver; he drove in a professional series like myself. I decided at a slower portion of the track I would slow down considerably in a turn and "conveniently" let him pass. Now I was following him. I watched as he took the uphill to see if and when his tires were slipping because of the dampness. This would allow me to make any necessary adjustments. It also had the benefit that I could follow his tracks. So now I had him as the point person and I also had my own feel of the car, putting me in the catbird seat. I knew if he could navigate the track, so could I.

We can apply this approach to events in everyday life. We can be patient and watch others trailblaze, since there may not be any real need to be first or incur risk unnecessarily. The key is to find a way to control our instincts and be patient.

In the end, judgment and patience can assist us in making sound decisions across many different environments and situations.

10

Racing at Night and Being Exhausted but Alert

"To learn something new, you need to try new things and not be afraid to be wrong."

Roy T. Bennett

"I often think that the night is more alive and richly colored than the day."

Vincent Van Gogh

M any believe that it's more complicated to drive a racecar at night than during the day. This is not necessarily the case. In daylight, our field of vision is very broad. In our peripheral vision, we see not only the track surface and the corner stations but also trees, grass, etc. At night, our field of vision tends to be more focused. This is partially a function of our headlights only illuminating a portion of what's ahead of us. Because we are more focused, driving at night can actually be easier than driving during the day. In racing, it helps that racecar headlights are bright and more effectively focus the driver's attention.

Most racetracks have spots that are not well lit. But with other tracks, like Daytona, it's like daytime around the clock because the lights are so bright. Indeed, Daytona's track owners have to inform city officials whenever they are planning to run the lights because doing so is such a massive drain on the power grid. (The track and the city coordinate to assure there is enough capacity for everyone.) But at tracks lacking overhead lights, it is more difficult see apexes at night. In many instances, the track installs reflectors at the apexes to allow the drivers to focus and therefore hit these apexes.

Many things can distract drivers. First, we need to focus on where we are going—no small matter when we are traveling at speeds up to 180 mph. Next, we need to monitor our instruments. While these are not a major focus, they do require some attention. Fortunately, modern racecars have alarms to alert us to any looming hazards. The main things we tend to monitor are the shift lights and the gear position. At night we add things like the distraction of the headlights.

In 2021, we were entered to race in the 24 Hours of Daytona. To prepare, we entered another race at Daytona that was part of a different series and included some night racing. In fact, there were four one-hour races—one at 5 p.m., one at 10 p.m., one at 5 a.m., and one at 10 a.m. This was intended to prepare us for driving at night, driving with minimal sleep, and driving with other faster cars on the same track in the same race. These were similar conditions to those we would be experiencing in the twenty-four-hour race. This also prepared me for the distractions caused by the headlights and the faster cars—often much faster—passing us.

Night racing can trigger situations that are almost impossible to believe. In 2006, we were in a thirteen-hour race at Virginia International Raceway. We had four drivers. I was the second fastest, just behind Carlos, whose brother Alberto was part of the crew. At one point during the night portion of the race, Carlos was driving and was off his pace. I was not around the pits since my turn in the car was about an hour away. I was going into the bathroom when the car owner's wife stopped me and asked, "Can you get in the car?" She said something was wrong with Carlos. I quickly went to the bathroom and put on my racing gear, and she drove me to the pits in the golf cart. Carlos pitted and I got in the car. I noticed a gas smell. It seemed Carlos was succumbing to the fumes. I probably should have refused to drive, but I decided to press ahead.

The car had two fuel tanks—a main tank and a reserve tank. Once the main tank was low, you turned on the transfer pump, which transferred fuel from the reserve tank to the main tank. There must have been something wrong with the fuel lines between the two tanks. The car was not ventilating the fumes properly and Carlos was being affected. The cockpit was not well lit. I could see the normal instrumentation just fine, but I couldn't see the dashboard very well, so I had to fumble around, with coaching from my crew, to open the vents and bring cool air into the cockpit. Even so, I could smell the fumes.

After a radio discussion with the crew, I determined that the fumes were present while the transfer was occurring. I decided the wisest course was to run the transfer pump for a lap or a lap and a half and then shut it off for two laps. This would allow the accumulated fumes to evacuate. The strategy worked and everything returned to normal. We finished in the top five—a good result. But Carlos did not make out so well. He was hospitalized overnight because of the prolonged exposure to the fumes.

The lesson here is clear: you never know what you're getting into until you're in it. Then you need to figure out what the issues are on the fly and quickly adapt. There's a semi-famous Mike Tyson quote: "Everyone has a plan until they get punched in the mouth." That idea applies here.

11

You're Driving with Your Mirrors

"The past is just data. I only see the future."

Ayrton Senna

"Keep your face always toward the sunshine—and the shadows will fall behind you."

Walt Whitman

In racing you must maintain a clear focus on where you are going. Remember, ocular driving means that you must look where you are going and not at what's right in front of you. Because where you look is where the car goes. Most traffic accidents are caused by drivers losing concentration or failing to look where they are going. Any distraction can mean a loss of concentration and can potentially spell disaster.

Race divers need to be fully aware of their environment and concentrate on what they are doing and where they are going. This will determine their success. If racers mess up one corner, they must not dwell on the mistake. They need to decipher what went wrong, but they can't afford to get bogged down with the error. The next corner is quickly approaching; focusing too much on the last one means risking another mistake.

In competition, there is also the problem of racing for position. The driver needs to be aware of passing and being passed. If there are competitors right behind you, you need to know who they are, where they are, and what they might do to get around you. One way to get around competitors is to hound them until they make a mistake. This is something like a forced error. If the driver is looking in their mirrors—racecars generally have a rearview mirror and two side mirrors—then they can't be looking ahead to where they are going. This will invariably lead to a forced error and a pass.

The same thing can happen in life. If you focus too much on something that has just happened to you, then you do not have a clear picture of what may happen next. Consider students who get a bad grade in school. It is appropriate for them to analyze why that happened. However, they must not dwell on the analysis. Suppose they have another test the next day. If they are hung up on the poor grade from the test the day before, it's likely they will have a poor showing in the second one. They need to analyze the first test and quickly ascertain whatever corrective action is needed, then move on.

Many of us focus too much on the negative aspects of what has occurred in the past. It's not that we are inclined to look on the dark side, but rather that those aspects seem to crowd out other things. Like in driving a racecar, we need to quickly move on to the next corner. At the same time, we need to remember key details so that we can analyze them once we've exited the car. This also applies to mistakes we have made in our lives, such as in jobs or relationships.

Another risk is overanalyzing the incident when we have the time. We can get swept up into what Tom Peters called the "paralysis of analysis." Too much analysis may lead to poor or poorly timed decisions.

The best strategy is to recognize the things that go wrong, but to quickly analyze the situation, take what you can from it, see what corrective actions are possible or necessary, and move on to the next situation. If time allows—usually offline and out of the field of battle—analyze the condition but resist the temptation to spend too much time on your reflections. In this context "too much time" can be a relative term, so use caution in how it is interpreted.

"Driving with your mirrors" means that you are focusing too much on what's behind you and not what's in front you—where you are going or want to go. Remember that the future is forward, not behind. If you dwell too much on the past or prior mistakes, you will tend to make another or even the same mistake again. The best approach is to quickly evaluate things that have occurred and then make a commitment to correct them in the future. Always focus forward.

There is an old saying: "Don't pay too much attention to the past, there's no future in it." Always remember: Objects in mirrors are *behind* you. They will stay behind you *if* you focus forward. Learn from the past—insights, mistakes, successes, etc.—but always focus forward. *Always.*

12

I Love It When a Plan Comes Together

"Live as brave men; and if fortune is adverse, front its blows with brave hearts."

Marcus Tullius Cicero

We plan for everything at the racetrack. We try to anticipate the weather and how we need to respond to its changes. We plan for everything around us. When it comes to the race, we try to anticipate what things will be like when the green flag drops.

One time we were racing for the championship at Summit Point Raceway, but we had qualified fourth. It was good—but not as good as being on the front row. The car that we were racing against for the championship was on the pole and there was another car on the outside pole that happened to be another car from our team. The car on the inside of the second row (our row) was in our class and fast. Before the race, we tried to anticipate literally everything that all of the competitors could or would do. The speed of the start, what gear they would start in, what each one would do on the start, what their respective reactions would be to the choices made by others, and so on.

We had set out a plan that called for us to pass the car on the inside of the second row (next to us), which would block him in the first turn, which was a sharp right. Then we would be able to get inside of the car on the outside pole (our teammate) in order to have the best possible track position for the right-hand turn. This would place us immediately behind the pole setter—the car we were racing for the championship.

According to the plan, we would then run down the pole setter and pass him at the exit of Turn 1 and before Turn 2, which was a spot where our car was better than his car (different cars have different handling characteristics and are better on different portions of a track). Once we had passed him, we would pull away along a section of the track where we knew we could outperform him. At that point, we would have about a three-car-length lead with only 80 percent of the first lap completed. Then we would be able to extend our lead as the cars behind us raced each other for position.

Even though our plans rarely work exactly as we expect, we nonetheless go through the process of making them. We also plan for all sorts of contingencies, some of which only have the remotest chance of occurring. But we plan.

Why do we plan? Doing so helps us anticipate the various circumstances and situations that could arise. The planning process also gives us confidence that we can navigate through when unexpected things do occur. Typically, only one or two of the twenty things we anticipate actually take place. However, these plans give us a sense of control. So we continue to plan and anticipate for the circumstances that *may* occur. You never know how things may work out. But even if they don't, we will at least feel like we anticipated things better.

In this particular race, everything worked out *exactly* as we anticipated. We in fact passed the inside second-row car, and even the outside pole setter, which left us on the pole setter's bumper at the end of the first straight. We passed him on the next turn and pulled away from him along the tighter section of the track. Then we managed to extend our lead for the entire race. Our teammate did his part and was able to get past the pole setter. This was the *only* time our entire plan rolled out precisely as we had anticipated. But it was fantastic.

So continue to plan. You never know—it could actually work out.

13

Patience, Discipline, Self-Awareness, and Self-Confidence: Have Them and Know When to Use Them

"With self-discipline, almost anything is possible."

Theodore Roosevelt

"Discipline is choosing between what you want now, and what you want most."

Abraham Lincoln

"Optimism is the faith that leads to achievement. Nothing can be done without hope and confidence."

Helen Keller

There is a track outside Cleveland called Nelson Ledges that I've always liked, probably because I always performed well there. (I had also convinced myself that I was not that good at my home track—Summit Point, in the West Virginia panhandle— so I went elsewhere.)

One weekend at Nelson Ledges, I was in a race that included one of my strongest competitors, a guy named Jerry. He had beaten me in other races, but never at Nelson Ledges. In this race I qualified P1, but he was just behind me in P2. A recent rainstorm had left some parts of track damp, though most of it was dry. In this particular race, I was competing with Jerry for the Kryder Racing Championship.

I led through the first two turns, but Jerry was right on my bumper. The next turn, a left-hander, had a wet spot. We usually entered that corner from the far right, but since he was on my tail I took a defensive line and stayed toward the left with one car width off the edge of the track. That way, if Jerry went through the wet spot he would have less traction and would likely spin out.

I figured wrong. Jerry went through the limited space I had left and he managed to make the turn. Because he was going so fast, he got ahead of me and made the pass. I was disappointed, but nonetheless impressed that he had made it work. Thereafter, I just stuck with him.

Each lap I tried to pass him at various corners of the track, but I didn't really want to pass at those points. When you attempt to make a pass, the other driver usually moves to a more defensive position to prevent you from doing so. With many drivers, these situations are gentlemanly and the racing is close but fair, without consequence (this is the case with most folks we race with but not all—some you can trust others you can't). Jerry was a clean racer.

My attempts at passing were just my way of finding out how he would respond. Because he got in front so early in the race, I had a lot of time to figure out how he was taking the turns and see where my car was better than his on the various sections of the track. I eventually developed a plan for passing him in a specific spot: three turns from the end of the lap.

The strategy worked. I passed him on the final lap—three turns from the finish—and won the race. If I had passed him earlier, he could have figured out how to pass me back.

After the race, Jerry and I talked. He said it was the most grueling race he had ever driven in, since he needed to worry about where I was at literally every moment of every lap. This was my precise strategy—bug the hell out of him and get on his nerves so he would make a mistake and miss something.

In similar life situations, we all want to try to get things done quickly—sometimes too quickly. We need to remember that choosing to take no action may be the correct decision, but the timing of that decision is critically important too. So we should not rush our decisions. Instead, we should honestly evaluate our relative position and our capabilities.

Making decisions too early in the above situation would have allowed Jerry to follow me and figure out my strategy. We were so close in lap times, I was sure he would have been right on my tail. I was also driving a little under what my car would do. In racing, it's often said that you run as fast as you can when qualifying, but in the race you run just fast enough to win.

Because I was following, I could see where I was at my best on the track. This enabled me to make the best decision. Whether I should have waited until the last lap is a fair question, and perhaps I should have built in a little more of a cushion. But the strategy worked and I won the race. The episode showed the power of patience—with a dose of self-confidence.

14

Reaction Time

"Do what you can, with what you have, where you are."

Theodore Roosevelt

"The world is moving so fast these days that the man who says it can't be done is generally interrupted by someone doing it."

Elbert Hubbard

"I'm a great believer in luck, and I find the harder I work the more I have of it."

Thomas Jefferson

In anything we do, we need to think about the goal we want to achieve. Once the goal is identified, we need to determine the resources needed and then develop a plan to achieve the goal, along with any related action steps.

This process involves identifying "what" we want to achieve, developing the plan, identifying the applicable action steps or tasks necessary to achieve the goal, beginning implementation of the plan's action steps, continually evaluating the plan, changing the plan as indicated, redeveloping actions, implementing the new actions and redeploying, and continuing that cycle until the goal is attained—or until it has been modified given new information. However, sometimes unanticipated things cause us to rethink and change course altogether.

On some occasions, we don't have time to rethink in the true sense of that word. We just need to react to the situation and hopefully we make the right or appropriate decision(s).

In 2007, I was in a thirteen-hour race at Virginia International Raceway (VIR). During a night stint, I was coming up on a car that was in the same class. In the back section of VIR's track there are no lights, and you can't see very much other than your headlights and the headlights of other cars. While I was catching the car in front of me, I also needed to make a pit stop in the next 2–3 laps. In other words, there was no need to race him and risk anything. I just needed to get by if it was possible to do so. However, in an endurance race you must never forget the goal, which is simply to finish the race. There may be several hours remaining, which was the case here, so it would have been shortsighted to risk damage to the car.

At one point I was coming down the back straight at about 130–140 mph and I was right on my competitor's tail. I couldn't see anything other than the back of his car. My high beams were on (which is normal) and I was getting reflection off the back of his white car, but that was manageable. We were on the racing line, which was on the right since at the end of the back straight is a left-hand sweeper. Suddenly, his car swerved quickly to the left to avoid a car that was sitting dead on the track. I swerved as well and we both managed to skirt past the car without incident and without slowing very much. Had either one of us hit that car, things would have gotten pretty ugly, really quickly.

At the end of the straight, I could tell that the driver of the car I was following was noticeably shaken by the experience. He overslowed for the corner (more so than during his previous laps), and I thought of making a pass. However, I decided that this was not the best time or place to try it, particularly since I was coming up for a pit stop again in the next lap or so. I radioed the crew and told them to remind me to tell them what had just happened on the back straight.

In life, we also have surprises like the one I just described. When they occur, we need to reflect but also have confidence in our abilities. My confidence made it possible for me to calmly turn the wheel to avoid the stopped car. This was a product of my training and experience. Drivers with less experience often make worse choices. Had my swerve been sharper, it's likely my car would have flipped.

We also need to be calm and return to our rhythm right away. I elected not to make the pass at the end of the straight given that the timing was bad and the driver was likely recounting the experience—a distraction for him. While I could have and would have leveraged this had the circumstances been different, the time wasn't right. We need to be confident in our abilities, remain calm, and make good judgment calls. That will get us through life's problems.

I also have a very different perspective about making quick but "good" decisions. In 2020, we were racing at Road Atlanta in the

International GT series. We were racing with a few friends who were on the same team—we help each other out when needed. One of the drivers on our team, Mark, was in our race but in a class above us. About one-third of the way through the race, the faster cars (which included Mark) started lapping other slower cars. Mark was leading his class and was coming up on a slower car going into Turn 6 at a mid-speed corner (about 80 mph). It was a right-hand turn that is immediately followed by another right-hand turn (this one very slow), which leads onto a mile-long straightaway with plenty of time to pass.

Approaching the slower car, Mark saw a gap between the right side of the car and the grass. Once he committed to venture into that opening, he saw the slower car turn to the right (which meant that car did not see him) and he moved to the right, which caused him to have two wheels on the grass and two wheels on the track. He hit the brakes and lost control, going straight instead of turning. The slower car tapped him in the left rear, which changed his trajectory toward the left. This placed him directly in the path of the car he was racing. That car hit Mark's left-side door and fenders and they both slid into the gravel trap, then collided with the wall on the right side of Mark's car. This ended the race for both cars, which were left with considerable damage. Repairing them was going to be a very expensive proposition, since both were in the "fastest class."

During the incident, Mark's helmet struck the upper side of the roll cage bar, which caused us to worry that he might have been left with a concussion. Fortunately, that wasn't the case and both drivers came away uninjured. But Mark had a huge dent in his ego—and his pocketbook.

Events like this happen in life too. We need to be sure we're not putting ourselves in the wrong position or situation. A better play in this situation would have been to go to the left and wait behind the slower car, thus placing Mark's car in a defensive position and blocking the competitor with whom he was racing. Alternatively, he could have made a pass entering the subsequent right-hand corner or just waited until he was on the straightaway, which would have been the safest bet. But he erred in assessing that the slow car saw him, ignoring that that car likely had stopped looking at his right-side mirror and was focused on the apex of the corner he was entering.

We can make these errors in judgment by failing to view the situation clearly. We must keep ourselves calm and focused. Mark was likely overly focused on the car behind and trying to keep him there. This caused him to lose focus on what he was doing in entering the corner. There were several other choices Mark could have made; he simply made the wrong one. He should have chosen the safer option. Had it been the last lap of the race, it may have been worth the risk—but last lap heroics should be saved for the last lap. This is all part of the risk-versus-reward scenarios we encounter in racing and in life.

To be successful, you need to react as situations evolve—and on occasion you need to react very quickly. Our reactions in these situations influence the outcome of our plans and goals. Anyone can make correct choices given infinite time and analytics. However, if you need to react quickly, as we increasingly do, you need to rely on what you know, which—as the first example above showed—are your training and instincts.

15

Only Perfect Practice Makes Perfect

"Perfection is not attainable, but if we chase perfection we can catch excellence."

Vince Lombardi

You're probably familiar with the saying "practice makes perfect." The theory is that if you want to be good at something, you need to practice that activity in order to become better at it. But nothing could be further from the truth.

When I was first learning the basics of racing, I was pretty adept at executing on the instruction I was receiving. That led me to be able to drive progressively faster. I even set some track records.

Only later did I discover that my initial instruction was incomplete—and in retrospect, some of it even seems to have been misguided. I came to learn about things like managing the car's weight, and that if you've slowed down too much while taking a turn you wait until you're through the turn to apply the throttle. I also learned big picture things, like a philosophical view of racing. What does it take to be fast (fast lap times)? Does the lap time come from the straightaways or the corners? (Answer: the corners!)

For most tasks we undertake, there is a correct way to perform them. Of course, for many of these things there is some personalization involved. They can and should be adapted to our personal style. But there is a correct way of doing these things within certain boundaries. Accordingly, practicing a suboptimal method or approach will not necessarily translate to a meaningful improvement in performance.

We need to understand the correct way of doing things in order to practice them the right way. Practicing the wrong way will only result in flawed approaches becoming part of our muscle memory (literally and figuratively). Indeed, it will become the only approach or technique that we understand. Just as damaging, we will convince ourselves that our motions are the right ones. As a result, we are unable to recognize the negative aspects of the behavior. It therefore becomes more difficult to change, even after we recognize the need.

If we adopt a bad behavior or technique, it will be 1) more difficult to recognize the negative aspects of the behavior, and 2) more difficult to change that behavior because the bad behavior is what is imprinted on our brains. Once we have carried out a task over and over again, we believe that the way we are doing it is the best way, but it also becomes the only way we know how to do it. Change depends on undoing what our brain knows as good behavior and then retraining ourselves and our brains for a new and different behavior. The longer we have been doing the bad behavior, the more difficult it will be to change it.

This is why we need to adopt good techniques and behaviors early. It is equally important that we practice those good techniques or behaviors. This is particularly true with racing. Bad techniques can be acquired early in a career and they can become embedded in our behaviors. Changing these behaviors often requires the help of others.

This lesson also applies to other aspects of our lives. Poor techniques in business or in work habits can have the same impact. Acquiring good techniques and behaviors early will minimize the changes we need to make later.

16

The Line Changes over Time: Plans Change

"Success is not measured by what you accomplish, but by the opposition you have encountered and the courage with which you have maintained the struggle against overwhelming odds."

Orison Swett Marden

When driving racecars, the track has a theoretical racing line. This is the classic path around the track, which considers the radii and camber in the turns as well as the entries and exits. However, tracks age and change over time. And those changes can force us to modify how we are driving. Therefore, we must change our approach to the line—or change the line itself. Those who figure out these changes sooner will be ahead of those who don't.

Our team had high hopes for the 2017 season, and we were planning to enter two cars in the series. Our approach was to enter two cars and practice with two cars, but only race one (the car I was driving). But the series changed the rules on us and made us start both cars in the race. We didn't want to race both cars. We decided to start the second car, which a member of our team (Hugh) would drive, then once we got to the pit stop we would simply park that car.

During the January 2017 race at Daytona, Hugh asked if I wanted to finish the car he started in, since this would mean more practice time. I told Hugh that I didn't feel that I was physically fit enough to do that, but it was a good thought. Six months later, we were racing at Watkins Glen, New York. When I exited my car, I felt great physically. It seemed that my continued physical conditioning program was paying off. I told Hugh about it and said I thought I could finish with his car.

"Great, let's plan on that," he said.

Each year in early July, our race series goes to Canada to race at the Canadian Tire Motorsports Park (known as Mosport). We generally travel to Canada immediately after racing at Watkins Glen.

One week after the Watkins Glen race in July 2017, we were racing our Porsches at Mosport and the track had a test day before the series event started. Hugh was driving one of our two cars. He was coming down the long back straight and at the end he needed to slow down to take the right-hand turn. But the brakes had gone out. He steered straight but with a slight right-hand tilt and crashed into the tire wall. While he was not injured, the car was badly damaged and could not be repaired in time for the race. We worked to identify the cause, which turned out to be a part failure. This type of failure leads directly to our parts replacement approach, which is based on the anticipated time the parts would wear out. We replace them before they fail to prevent this from happening. Fortunately, Hugh was okay.

During practice the next day, I was driving our other car and going through the sequence of turns where the brakes went out on Hugh. As I was getting ready to make the slowish right-hand turn onto the front straight, my car was tapped in the rear. That tap was at such a force and angle that my car was forced to abruptly turn left and I collided directly with a concrete wall at 50–60 mph. While still in the car, my right leg didn't feel right. When I was assisted getting out of the car, it could not bear any weight.

In racecars we do not have power brakes to assist us with brake modulation while making turns. Therefore, if we want 1,600 pounds of brake pressure on the pedal, our right leg makes it happen. When I hit the concrete wall, I was still trying to stop and things happened so fast that I could not get my foot off the brake pedal. According to the car's data, the brake pressure went to 3,000 pounds. My Achilles tendon could not take that much pressure, which resulted in my tendon being severed. Needless to say, the team was concerned about my condition but also devastated since we had lost two cars in twenty-four hours.

After the medical personnel at the track examined me, I was transported to the hospital. I was examined and had X-rays taken. They told me they would normally do a CT scan but they couldn't because it was a Friday, which tells you something about Canada's health care system. It was clear that I needed surgery, but I didn't want to get it in Canada. They put my right leg in a cast, gave me some pain medications, and sent me back to the track.

Later that day, I called my doctor and told him what happened and that I would likely need orthopedic surgery. He said to call the office when I got back. He knew who to call since the year earlier he had had an injury skiing and needed orthopedic surgery. I waited around the next day at the track and then flew home—with cast and crutches. The team was great pulling things together and dealing with the carnage and carting me to the airport.

In a week or so, I had Achilles surgery to reattach the severed tendon. Here I am in a cast and in pain. How did I get here? From the great physical conditioning and getting ready to finish Hugh's car, now I couldn't race. I couldn't drive at all since it was my right leg that was affected. How did this happen?

After months of therapy and a continued physical fitness program, I was back in a racecar in November. At my direction, the team got Hugh to drive with my co-driver and they finished the season that way. I attended all the races cheering them on. So the show didn't stop—it continued even though we had a big problem.

The message here is that I had a great plan that I was getting ready to execute. Then something unexpected changed everything, in a pretty dramatic way. I was left immobile and injured, my fitness program was impaired, my track time was affected, and because I couldn't drive, my driver development stopped in its tracks.

We developed work-arounds to get me back in a car in the shortest time possible. I got a full reattachment surgery rather than just a repair. A full reattachment was the only way to get back to 100 percent so I could drive racecars again. The physical therapist gave me conditioning exercises to do when in and not in therapy. I continued my other exercise program too. We worked around having only two drivers and we even had a work-around to get me through the airports.

As the song says, "ain't no stopping us now."

17

Focus on What *You* Can Do to Improve Your Situation

"Very little is needed to make a happy life; it is all within yourself, in your way of thinking."

Marcus Aurelius

About nine months after I had the Achilles tendon surgery, I was driving and racing again. On a trip home from a track in Florida, I had a connecting flight through Atlanta. Before boarding the first flight, I saw a guy wearing a neck brace. He had walked up to the counter and asked the agent, "I guess you're wondering why I'm wearing this neck brace?" Then, without hesitation, he told the attendant that he'd had an accident about 9–10 months earlier, was still in great pain, and was in jeopardy of becoming paralyzed if he didn't wear the brace.

As he boarded the plane, he said to the attendant scanning his boarding pass, "I guess you're wondering why I'm wearing this neck brace?" He then told her the same story of potentially being paralyzed.

He was sitting two rows in front of me. When the flight attendant asked if he wanted something to drink, he ordered and then said, "I guess you're wondering why I am wearing this neck brace?" And then proceeded to tell the same story.

When at the gate for my connecting flight, the same individual came up to the counter—this time in a wheelchair—and asked the attendant behind the counter, "I guess you're wondering why I'm wearing this neck brace?"

I had a window seat on the flight. Just my luck, this guy was in the aisle seat right next to me. He looked at me and says, "I guess you're wondering why I'm wearing this neck brace?" I politely didn't respond, but he still told me the same story.

He harped on the fact that his neck hurt when he moved it. I asked why he didn't get physical therapy. He responded that he did go to physical therapy but that it involved moving his neck, and sometimes that hurt. I told him that I drove racecars professionally and told him to look at my right leg and foot. I then rotated my right ankle (the one that had the severed Achilles months before). I told him, "Nine months ago, my right Achilles tendon was severed in a racing accident in which I crashed directly into a concrete wall. I had surgery and went to physical therapy. And yeah, the surgery and therapy were painful, but I did it. And you know why I did it? Because I wanted to drive racecars again. In fact, I'm returning from driving racecars right now." I went on to tell him, "If you don't like your therapist, then change therapists. But you need to realize that the physical therapists are trying to help you. You need to, *in fact you must*, make the commitment to do your part. If you don't, you won't get better." He didn't talk to me the rest of the trip.

As they say in running, "the race is not always to the swift but to those that keep on running." The key is to keep running and stay focused on our goals.

18

A Changing Environment Requires Changing Solutions, Actions, and Commitment

"It is no use saying, 'we are doing our best.' You have got to succeed in doing what is necessary."

Winston Churchill

"Always make a total effort, even when the odds are against you."

Arnold Palmer

"There is no limit to what a man can do or where he can go if he does not mind who gets the credit."

Ronald Reagan

DAYTONA

One week in November 2020, we were racing at Daytona International Speedway. We had high expectations for our 2015 modified Porsche GT3 Cup car. This event had the potential to be a big contributor to our success in the International Motor Sports Association (IMSA) 24 Hours of Daytona race a few months later in February.

We selected the Porsche because its attributes were like those of the car we would race in Daytona. We would also be getting thoroughly comfortable with the track through lots of track time. There were many 25–30 minute sprint races and practices spread across the six days of the event and one final event, the Classic 24 Hour race. It is not a single race, but rather four one-hour races spread across twenty-four hours. This latter race had other components we were interested in. It involved racing at night, which is an experience in and of itself (discussed earlier). We were also drawn to racing tired. We were to have one-hour races at 5 p.m., 10 p.m., 5 a.m., and 10 a.m. This event was tailor-made for us, given what we were hoping to achieve in January.

But during one of the sprint races, I made a mistake and clipped a curb in a high-speed section of the track. I overcorrected, which caused the car to spin around and slide backwards into a guardrail, damaging the right side. While I was okay, the car needed considerable work to get it back on the track. In fact, we would later find out that the chassis could not be repaired. We did not know that at the time, but we knew we could not race that car.

We brainstormed and came up with the idea of retrieving another of our cars that was like the one that was damaged. There was a problem though. The car was at another team's shop in

Chattanooga, Tennessee. We talked to the other team owner, who was racing at another track, and attempted to get some of their guys to bring the car to us in one of their trailers. Another option was to get a truck and trailer from our shop in Orlando, which was about one hour away, and the two would meet somewhere in the middle.

That team could not get a driver to their shop in time, so we decided to have one of our team members from the Orlando shop put his personal car in one of our trailers, bring our truck and trailer to us in Daytona, unload his car, and drive back. This way we had an empty truck and trailer to get the other car, and our Daytona team had a truck and trailer to use.

Once we had the truck and trailer, we put the wrecked car into the trailer to take to the Chattanooga shop for repair. We were going to drop the wrecked car and pick up our other car. We had two of our team members volunteer to go to Chattanooga and retrieve the car—a ten-hour trip each way.

They arrived in Chattanooga at 11 p.m. Our guys met the other team's crew, who had prepared our other car while our guys were in transit. The guys swapped the damaged car for our other car, picked up a few parts, and took off back to Daytona. They arrived back in Daytona around 10 a.m. and immediately started to get the car ready. The two volunteers had kept us updated and we had breakfast ready for them when they arrived. By 1:30 p.m., the car was prepped, tech'ed, fueled, and ready to go. It was on the track in time for the 2:30 p.m. practice session. It ran well and we finished the race in fifth place. A great achievement and great experience given that endurance races are a test of both man and machine.

The test of a great team is not in the individual achievements of the individual team members. While this is important from the perspective of the quality of the team members, what's really important is how the team adapts to adversity. By that I mean how a team comes together as a team and does what it takes to get the job done—whatever that job might be and whatever that job entails. The two guys who drove to Chattanooga and back made a great sacrifice because they recognized we came to do a job, which was to race. Race we did—and we did it well. These two crew members never questioned what needed to get done. They just did it.

This is what we can learn from in life. You could sit around and complain about everything: your job, the long hours, fatigue, who should go, etc. But it is the selfless focus on performance, coupled with the job that needs to get done, that leads to results.

This goes for all of us on the team. While drivers get a lot of the credit, we cannot do what we do without the team. When it was my turn to get back into the car at 10 a.m. for the last race, I was tired. I had driven at 5 a.m. and had only gotten three-and-a-half hours' rest. But I got back in and drove the full one-hour stint. That was my contribution to what we all had committed to accomplish.

ROAD ATLANTA

I was supposed to race at Road Atlanta in an endurance race one weekend with some of my teammates. At the time, we were racing BMWs. My co-driver arrived early for the sprint races. I had to travel a day later because I needed to give a talk in Asheville, North Carolina, for my professional association. I towed the endurance car in a trailer with me. The plan was for me to use the sprint races as practices and not really race since I had missed the test day.

I arrived feeling cheery on Saturday and approached my team. I saw my co-driver's car parked behind his trailer, which was sort of unusual. The car of one of my other teammates was on jack stands, but I thought nothing of it. There was another car being worked on that usually races with us, as we were all friends.

"Hey guys how's it going?" I asked.

The first teammate I ran into was waving his hands in a downward direction as if to say "pipe down."

"What's up?" I asked.

He said that my co-driver's car had blown a motor and the other car on jack stands had hit a wall pretty bad. Neither car could be repaired in time to race.

"You mean I have the only car that works?" I said.

To which he responded, "Yup."

So, I went out and practiced in the sprint race, as planned. During one lap I was going down a mile-long straight when I heard something go wrong with the motor. At first, I thought it was running out of fuel, but it had plenty. Then I looked in the mirror and saw tons of blue smoke coming out the rear, which meant I had a blown motor. I radioed in and they accused me of missing a shift, which would have blown the motor. I responded that when the motor went, I had been in fifth gear a long time so a missed shift was unlikely. We agreed to just relax and watch some races—essentially give up, accept the situation, and have fun.

But one of the guys said there was a BMW junkyard about four miles down the road and suggested we go there to see if they might have a motor. I went with my co-driver and when we arrived, I asked if they had a motor for our car. Not only did they have a motor, but it was already out of the car and had low miles. We bought it on the spot and loaded it into the bed of the pickup, along with some other parts he had for sale.

Since we had so many incapacitated cars, we had plenty of folks to work on our endurance car—it was the only one that had a chance of racing. After about five hours, we had the motor in the car. We then sourced some oil from other competitors and got the thing running. It ran for a while so we shut it off and declared victory. We now had a running car. We changed the oil again since we didn't know how long the motor had been sitting. The next day we raced and finished on the podium—second as I recall. We had met our objective.

Here again we regrouped, thought through our options, and figured out a new strategy. It wasn't the initial plan, but we were able to get back to the objective—compete in the endurance race on Sunday. Once back in focus, we were able to leverage the assets we had available and achieve a level of success that was pretty impressive given where we were and what we had to work with.

The key is to focus only on what needs to get done. We can discuss the process and the tasks; but once the decision is made, follow the guidance of Nike: "Just Do It."

19

The Laws of Physics Apply in Racing and Life

"Attitude is a little thing that makes a big difference."

Winston Churchill

The laws of physics apply to virtually all aspects of life. Because the laws are based on proven facts, they are not in dispute. Therefore, one can live by certain basic premises that are also proven constants, and when one needs a frame of reference for something, it is comforting to know that the premises upon which you are relying are correct. These premises can also serve as unyielding, indisputable principles that can be used as a philosophical reference point for living one's life.

BODIES IN MOTION

Let's use Newton's Third Law of Motion as an example. This law says that once momentum is initiated and movement has begun, the mass will continue in motion until some other force acts on it to slow it down or change its course.

This also applies to life: Things that are screwed up then remain screwed up. And once things get out of whack, there is great difficulty in getting them corrected. That's because there is an undertow that creates inertia and keeps things locked in place. The issues that cause problems seem to be almost innate in many organizations and people. If you repeatedly do something the wrong way, such as your running technique or your eating patterns, then you are only practicing a bad habit.

How does this translate to racing? In Chapter 15 I discussed the saying "practice makes perfect." This is not an accurate statement. The truth is that only perfect practice makes perfect. For example, there is supposed to be only one perfect line through each corner of a racetrack and therefore around any given track. In racing, if you do not learn the correct technique at the onset, then you could be doing the wrong thing during the entire race. Racers on an incorrect line through the corners will keep driving that same line repeatedly. They will become perfect at driving that line. There's only one problem: it's the wrong line and it is not the fastest.

Experience tells us that the racing line we were taught is not really the fastest. It might have been the fastest initially, but the line can change because the track can change. The track pavement can change over time with age, it can be patched, or it can be replaced. Any or all of these changes can dictate a different faster line. The challenge is that we must adapt to the changes in the environment and make changes accordingly. Then we must constantly work to identify any changes in the environment and use them as a stimulus to change.

FOR EVERY ACTION, THERE IS AN EQUAL AND OPPOSITE REACTION

Let's discuss an example of what we are talking about here. Take Newton's Second Law of Motion: for every action there is an equal and opposite reaction. When a force acts on an object and generates movement, there will be an equal force in the opposite direction. For example, if you squeeze a balloon in the middle, the force applied acts to displace the air as pressure is applied and that air transfers the force into an opposite reaction, forcing the air to push out of the balloon at another spot.

This concept actually applies in life. It's quite similar to "what goes around comes around." That even sounds like Newton's law. Translated, it means that what you do to others, others will do to you. This is something that you can rely on and count on. You should adopt this kind of philosophy for how you live your life. Treat others with same courtesy and respect that you would expect. That way all of us are being treated equally by one another.

This idea applies to the racecourse as well. If a driver shows no respect for other drivers, they will have no respect for him or her. Consider a few common situations: allowing someone enough "racing room," giving a car in another class space to pass while racing for position, or being too aggressive and tapping another car, which causes it to spin out. A driver's behavior in these situations will shape how that driver is viewed by others. Then when the opportunity presents itself, the driver will be treated likewise. This can apply to even the most minor things, such as someone loaning you a tool or piece of equipment. If you have not been fair, open, and honest in your treatment of others, then it comes back to you, often in spades.

20

Passion: Let It Drive You but Not Control You

"If passion drives you, let reason hold the reins."

Benjamin Franklin

Passion is a key ingredient in everything you seek to accomplish. The more passion you have, the more you will throw yourself into the endeavor. Passion is your drive, your energy. It makes you want to be engaged. You exude energy from passionate pursuits.

I have passion for racing and for the pursuit of better treatments for cancer. Those passions make me want to devote my energies to each of these endeavors.

As we draw on the energy we derive from passion, we must be cautious about it as well. If it becomes extreme, it can crowd out other important things in your life. For example, I could be so passionate about my racing that I start skipping work. Or I could be so devoted to racing that it crowds out having a relationship with someone. This crowding out would be very unfortunate in that we all need these other dimensions in our lives to make us whole.

We need balance in our lives and that includes the physiological, financial, and emotional balance. This balance will help to make our lives whole.

21

Frustration: Expect It and Manage It

"Always make a total effort, even when the odds are against you."

Arnold Palmer

"Great spirits have always encountered violent opposition from mediocre minds."

Albert Einstein

"When everything seems to be going against you, remember that the airplane takes off against the wind, not with it."

Henry Ford

We always want things to go smoothly—whether it's a project at work, a drive to the airport, or anything else. But there are often stumbling blocks and potholes along the way.

Perhaps that's because we didn't plan correctly, or the environment changed, or something else. Oftentimes we think the world is conspiring against us. But it could just be random bad luck.

We can get flustered when things get complicated and many issues come at us simultaneously. There is an old joke that involves a patient talking to his psychiatrist:

Psychiatrist: Mr. Smith, I have great news. You are not paranoid.

Mr. Smith: Great.

Psychiatrist: Everybody really is out to get you.

We often feel like there's a conspiracy against us. Other times we want things to work a certain way, and when they don't we begin to have negative thoughts. As pressure mounts, we get more and more agitated. That never helps and it likely makes things worse.

My racing team has had countless experiences with our plans getting messed up for some reason. During a race start, we might have a plan for things to work a certain way, then there is a big accident in front of us and we're done for that day.

When our team was racing at Sebring in 2021, our car had been given a BOP (Balance of Performance) adjustment made by the race series to equalize the cars on the track that essentially slowed the car on the straightaways. So we developed a strategy that was based on a fuel mileage approach. A slower car typically uses less fuel. If we could stop less, or have shorter stops, we would get back on the track sooner than our competitors, since their non-restricted motors would be burning more fuel.

When one of our drivers was nearing the third turn of the first lap, another racer hit his left rear wheel and damaged the axle. He limped back to the pits, and when the crew was finished we were about thirty laps down. We had no hopes of winning, but we wanted to get whatever points we could and stayed out until the race ended.

During the same race, the power steering unit failed in our other car after about fifteen laps. So the driver, Owen, drove it without power steering, which requires tons of arm and shoulder effort—not pleasant. Then he found that he couldn't turn the wheel as far as he needed, so he had to go slower through the corners until the speed of the car allowed it to turn. The result was a lot of cars passing him.

With both cars out of contention—one because of someone else and the other because of a part failure—we were pretty bummed and were starting to get frustrated. First the BOP adjustment, then the incident on the start, and then the part failure. To top things off, the winning car had the same strategy as our car that got dinged during the start. Given that we have better and faster drivers, there was a good chance we would have won the race. Instead, we were two races into the year and had few points to our name. We started wondering about our hopes for the championship. Suffice it to say, we were frustrated with the situation, with the series, and with just about everything.

Some ideas about how to handle situations like this come from the medical profession, where errors can have disastrous consequences. Unfortunately, medical errors do happen (they're one of the leading causes of death in the United States) and they are more prone to occur in the emergency room, where there can be many patients, each with different problems, who might all need attention at the same time.

In order to reduce diagnosis and practice errors, a team of medical researchers in Australia developed the following tips for emergency room physicians:

- Take two (take a breath and relax)
- Think (think through the available information in a calm manner)
- Then do (develop a plan of what to do while in a calm state, reflecting on the information available, or consider what other information is needed)

It's clear that we can pursue the right course of action if we concentrate on the information available to us and filter out the noise that distracts us. We can also determine what other information is needed to help improve our decision-making. This is contrary to the reality we're all familiar with, when we get so flustered that our brains can't focus properly and we make errors or the wrong decisions.

This applies to racing, but it also applies to many aspects of our lives. No matter how complicated things get, we generally have enough information to make the right decision. It's just that we don't focus, or can't focus, on that information when we need to. It could be that we need other perspectives because there are so many things occurring simultaneously. We may need others to provide ideas, or we might just need to slow the decision process down a little, which can help better ideas come to the fore.

How did we handle the disappointment at Sebring in 2021? We regrouped quickly and developed a plan for the remainder of the year, starting with our next race, which was six weeks away.

22

The Three Turns: Analysis, Focused Improvement Areas, and Execution

"Do not let what you cannot do interfere with what you can do."

John Wooden

Much of racing is based on data and analytics. In fact, the car provides data for a wide variety of variables. We can collect data about anything for which there are sensors. This includes throttle position, steering position, braking force, and timing.

In November 2020, we were at Road Atlanta. I was about 4 seconds per lap slower than one of my co-drivers, Hugh. When we compared our data, we found that 2.7 seconds of the four-second differential, or delta, was related to three turns. And our analysis showed that the lost time was slightly different for each turn. We concluded that if I focused on the three turns while working on not changing any of the other turns, we could close the gap. In an endurance race, a narrower gap would mean that who was in the car would matter less, and that the options for pit stops and drive time would be less of a factor. That, in turn, would open up the team's race strategy options.

Turn 3. The issue with Turn 3 was my braking; specifically, I was holding the brake too long. At our level, we use the brake for two purposes: 1) slowing the car and/or 2) putting weight on the outside front tire as we attempt to turn. But we generally don't do both at the same time or at the same rate. If we are doing the latter, once we get close to the apex of the turn it is important to release the brake, as this will allow the car to turn better. (In fact, the car doesn't like to turn with the brake on.) Once we release the brake, we can slow the car even more by using steering input, since turning the steering wheel creates friction and can slow the car. In this turn, it was my timing of the brake release coupled with my turn in that would scrub off some speed.

Turn 5. Drivers enter this turn after going full throttle downhill to the bottom; the braking area has a very slight rise. Here the analytics suggested that I was not holding full throttle long enough. Specifically, I needed to hold full throttle about 125 feet longer to be comparable to Hugh. In other words, I needed to target the end of the curbing as opposed to the 125-foot mark I must have been looking at. If I could do that, I would achieve an arrival speed into the turn similar to Hugh's.

We also saw that I needed to wait a little longer before I turned into the corner, which would translate into my being able to go back to the throttle sooner. Doing so would increase my exit speed down the following short straightaway. That increased speed would endure all the way down the straight. This could make a difference of about three car lengths at the end of a straight of reasonable length.

Once you lose exit speed, you can't recover it for the rest of the lap or the race. Generally, all track speed, either on the straights or through the corners, places one farther down the track than one's competitor. The result is better lap times and a greater likelihood of winning, which is the point.

Turn 6. In Turn 6, I was applying the brake a little too soon, similar to Turn 5. But I was also holding onto the brake a little too long, which was similar to what I was doing in Turn 3. The strategy here was to get closer to the brake marker into that turn. (Each turn generally has defined brake markers, measured in number of feet prior to the turn, such as 300', 200', 100'—or there are other physical attributes one can use as a reference point.)

I needed to carry more speed through the corner, which has a little camber in the center and thus allows for a bit more speed. But I wasn't using that camber as much as needed. The corner entry speed was important because it was immediately followed by a slow corner that I had to take in second gear. Since I was going toward a slower corner, maximizing the entry was more important than the exit.

Once we looked at this situation, we saw differences between Hugh and me but also many similarities in how I was approaching and handling the turns. These similarities were important because they impacted the number of changes that I needed to make. "Focus," as always, would be key to success. One can only do so many things at once. Therefore, the more limited the changes that needed to be made—assuming I took the other nine turns correctly—the more dramatically would the chance for a successful change to be implemented increase.

This applies in life too. Focus, focus, focus. If we focus on what we are attempting to accomplish and can isolate the particular things we have targeted, we can succeed. If we attempt to change too much all at once, we dramatically reduce our chance for success. Analytics helped us isolate and prioritize the possible changes and achieve success sooner.

This is precisely what we did at Road Atlanta. Hugh's performance gave us a built-in baseline. We could compare his data and mine in the same car, on the same day, literally minutes apart. This allowed us to identify the possibilities that made the most sense for achievement. Once the options or target behaviors were determined, the hard part began—executing those changes. Human behavior changes are the most difficult, even when you know they're needed to meet your goal. (Implementing these changes when you're going 160 mph and on a track with forty other cars doing the same thing only adds to the difficulty.) The key is identification, time, focus, determination, and tenacity—but it *can* be done.

23

Believing and Knowing You Can Do It Will Get You There: There Is No Try

"Try not. Do or do not. There is no try."

Yoda

The human brain does not understand "try." The word implies that failing to complete a task or meet a goal is a potential option. Those who use the word to describe something they are about to undertake also embrace the notion of failure or incompletion. For example, "I'll try to meet you on Tuesday at 5 p.m." My brain understands this as, "I'll work toward meeting you but if I don't it's somehow okay." Not completing something is a possibility.

The Empire Strikes Back (part of the *Star Wars* series) gives us an example of how negative notions can affect how we perform. In this movie, there is a scene where Luke Skywalker is stranded on a planet and his ship has sunk in a swamp. He is with Yoda, who was training Luke to use his Force. Luke concentrates on lifting the ship from the swamp and eventually says, "I can't. It's too big." Yoda responds, "Size matters not. Look at me. Judge me by my size do you?" Then Yoda lifts the ship out of the water.

Whether driving a racecar, or just pursuing any goal whatsoever, we need to believe we can do it. When a driver goes into a high-speed turn at 120 mph, he needs to "know" he can make it. Confidence is important, but it needs to be underpinned by the knowledge of having done the necessary prep to achieve the task at hand. That means having engaged in the "perfect practice" I referred to earlier. If you've done that, and believe in your ability, you are likely to achieve. Otherwise, you're just tricking yourself into being confident, and that's unlikely to pay dividends.

Targeting an accomplishment helps to achieve it. It's no coincidence that the most successful people tend to make lists. Preparing a list and then prioritizing it will focus one on tasks and on completing them.

We should all set goals. I have personal goals, financial goals, relationship goals, racing goals, etc. Goals get converted into tasks. Generally, the tasks are on the lists. I prepare a master list, but I also have a list for every day, including weekends. Then I prioritize the list and work at getting things accomplished. Even when I have items left on the list that were not accomplished, it doesn't bother me or demoralize me. The unfinished items are merely items for tomorrow or next week. Because I've prioritized, the important things are getting done.

When I look at my long lists, I'm not intimidated. I typically have tons of stuff to do, so prioritization and focus are critically important for me. Therefore, I prioritize the items on the list and see where I wind up. Whenever folks ask me to do something for them, I reflect on whether I can do it and have time, given the task and when they need it done. If I can do it and want to do it, then I'll commit to doing it. I tell these folks that if I commit to doing something, they should make sure I write it on the list. That way they will be sure I see it and I will be more likely to work the item into my day or my week. Most of what I commit to do, I do.

24

The Knowns and the Unknowns: Understand the Knowns and Be Ready to Deal with the Unknowns

"The man who moves a mountain begins by carrying away small stones."

Confucius

There are knowns and unknowns associated with any endeavor and racing is no different. You need to be prepared for many different scenarios—and adapt to the unexpected. There are several parallels between life experience and the endurance races in which I drive.

As the late former secretary of defense Donald Rumsfeld once put it, there are "known knowns," "known unknowns," "unknown knowns," and "unknown unknowns." While you can do a lot of planning for the "knowns," it's the "unknowns" that ultimately matter more.

By explanation, there are things we know we need to know, and we know what those things are and the related answers. There are other things we need to know but the answers are unknown to us. Then there are unknowns for which we know the answer but it is unknown to us that we need to know them or how and where they fit into the mix. Lastly, there are unknown things that we need to know, but we don't know we need to know them and we wouldn't know what those answers are if we did. These "knowns" and "unknowns" frame the context of this chapter's lessons.

In an endurance race there are knowns and unknowns. We know we will need to do things like change drivers, put on new tires, and add fuel. But with a long race, there is also a complex matrix of decisions that need to be made and there are many unknows, which include a range of potential failures: electrical, wipers, defroster, wires, and humans. Racing at night or in the rain adds unknown unknowns. It's really a matter of being prepared for the unexpected—and being able to respond and address those changes even in adverse situations, often with limited awareness of whether—or when — they will occur. Adapting to unknown unknowns and doing so quickly are keys to success. And adapting to adversity is the hallmark of a great team.

Our team was planning to race in the 24 Hours of Daytona at the end of January 2021. It is the biggest sportscar race in the country, and it was going to be the biggest race the team had entered. As such there were many unknowns, and we had to learn and identify those unknowns and their answers. We had a strategy for the events leading up to the race.

In December 2020, our team was at a different race in Daytona. We entered in order to get track time, but I (along with my teammates) was also in a four-way competition for the championship in the International GT Series. I was focused on winning the Porsche 3.8-liter class, but I also wanted track time as part of our preparations for the big race. Because of the COVID-19 pandemic, some races were cancelled and others were moved.

The best way to win a championship is to drive in all the races and do your best in each one (a known). Then if you underperform in some of the races (an unknown), you have a cushion.

In this series they count your ten best sprint races and your five best endurance races. The uncertainty about our position stemmed from not knowing how we would do (an unknown), how the others would do (an unknown), what races we would be able to drop (an unknown), and the races that would be dropped by our rivals (an unknown). None of these unknowns and knowns are fully understood until all the races are completed.

I was focused on beating the class leader, a driver named Bob. I wanted to beat Bob because he had the points lead and there were two others up there in addition to myself. I expected to do well at the prior race at Road Atlanta since it was my home track, but that's not what happened. I finished fourth in both sprint races and first in the endurance race. Bob had finished better than me in both sprint races (he was in the top three) and in doing so had enhanced his lead in the championship.

The series, recognizing they needed to assure they had enough races to calculate the race finishes, decided to make all the races at the Daytona event (the last one of the year) count as two races each. Plus, the Daytona event had three sprint races (instead of the normal two) as well as the endurance race. That meant there were effectively a total of eight races at the event—six sprint races (three races, each counting as two) and two endurance races (one endurance race that counted as two races). The number of races were knowns, but the outcomes were unknowns. All three of the sprint races were to be held on the same day—a long day for all of us. I needed to focus on doing as well as possible, and I certainly needed to finish ahead of Bob as much as possible. My focus was to do well and ignore the pressure to perform well.

I started the first sprint race from the fourth position. The race was dry and I managed to finish in second place, two positions ahead of Bob. (The guy who finished first was not a factor in the championship, as he had not run many races up until this point.) So now I had a second-place finish, which would ultimately count as two second places in the championship.

The next race was later in the day. Rain showers had come in and the track was wet, but not like a monsoon had come through. I expressed concern about rain racing to my endurance co-driver, Hugh, who responded, "you are pretty good in the rain."

"Maybe," I responded. "But rain racing is not my preference." The rain removed some uncertainty and converted an unknown into a less unknown.

But all of us were racing in the same conditions. I started on rain tires in second. On the start I pushed deeper into the first turn, which left a gap between me and the following cars. Just past the first turn, the first-place car in my class spun directly in front of me (an unknown) and it looked like he was going to stay to the right, so I thought of moving left to avoid him. But he moved left across the track, directly in front of me (an unknown). Because of the gap I had created, I was able to move right and not hit anyone. The other cars behind me were blocked slightly by the spun car, which was damaged and unable to continue. After that, I settled into a rhythm and proceeded to pull away from the rest of the cars in my class.

I had adapted to the wet conditions better than the others. It was one of the better races I have ever driven—and many others independently told me the same. (When the race was over, I couldn't even see the second-place car in my class.) Now I had a first-place finish, which really meant two first places. It seemed like things were coming together, championship-wise.

In the next race I started second again. It was a dry race. On the start, I moved to the inside left (a known) and managed to get by the first-place car going into turn one. He then got blocked because of an incident in front of him (both unknowns). His car was damaged and he was not a factor after that. Once again, I got into a rhythm and managed to win this race. Now I had one second place and two first places. Given the scoring system, with each race counting two races, I had two second places and four first places. Things were looking better. (The race wins given the circumstance were unknowns and the situation that evolved was also unknown.)

At this point, we were desperately trying to figure out the championship points—not only for me but for Bob and the two other guys. Our crude estimate was that I was now leading Bob by about eight points—a very narrow margin (an unknown).

When I started the endurance race, the track was dry. After a few laps, Tom (Bob's co-driver) managed to pass me. I was then in second place. Over the radio my crew told me not to contest the position because we did not want to risk damaging our car. We needed to finish this race, and since Hugh was faster than both Bob and Tom we knew he could make up lost track position (a known). After only a few laps Bob's brakes locked up and spun some distance in front of me (an unknown). Tom managed to regroup but I was now very close. He kept locking up the brakes, which suggested to me there was a problem with his car. With Bob's car now in my sights, I just stayed with him and was cautious in the event he locked up.

We were coming up on our pit stop in a few laps, but before I could stop Bob's car pitted. I was now in first place. Bob's car did not come out of the pits as expected, which suggested they had a problem that needed to be remedied. It also meant our first place was looking more likely (an unknown was becoming a known). Matt (another one of my co-drivers) had started the endurance race to test a few things on our Daytona 24 Hours car. Two laps after Bob's car pitted, I pitted and turned the car over to Hugh in first. As expected, Hugh drove a great race. Because our team had two cars running in the endurance race and I wanted more track time, I went two pits down and got into Matt's car when he pitted. Then I finished the race in that car and paid less attention to the results of the cars in the 3.8-liter championship race (because I was driving), but I knew we had won.

On the podium, they told me I had won the championship. However, I didn't just win the championship for my class. Instead, I won the championship for the entire Porsche IGT series for 2020 (an unknown). It seems that the championship was for all 3.8-liter Porsches, including the cars that were in faster classes than us. A driver in one of the upper-class cars was racing for the championship too. Unfortunately, very late in the race that car had a mechanical problem and retired. Little did I know, that helped me win the championship because that driver finished second in the championship and Bob finished third (an unknown). The second-place car in the championship would not have been a real factor in the points because he had not run enough races. The best he could do was second place, given what I had achieved.

This is a racing example of the "knowns" and the "unknowns." You analyze all you can up front to assess where things are. But as you begin to follow your initial strategy, you have to react as things unfold in front of you. However, if you focus, work on your plan, change and react, and recalculate as you go, you will wind up in a better position than you otherwise would have.

25

When Your Plans Explode, Regroup and Keep Moving

"Perseverance is not a long race; it is many short races one after another."

Walter Elliott

"There were a hundred ways we could have screwed this up, but we didn't."

Hugh Plumb

In February 2021, we were racing at an IGT race is Sebring, Florida. While there, I received my award for winning the IGT Championship Trophy in 2020. I was now ready to defend my championship.

We had our new IGT car rebuilt and ready to go. The car had a new tub, as well as a new motor that we had received from another very reputable Porsche team. The motor had been run on a dynamometer the same week and was making great power. Things were looking pretty good.

But on test day, Hugh, my co-driver, took the car out for a warmup lap and made it to the ninth turn (of seventeen) before the motor let go. It lost oil pressure at about Turn 9, so he shut it off immediately in order to salvage what he could. The car got towed back to the pit and the evaluation suggested we needed another motor. We searched but didn't find one.

We brainstormed and decided that we would go get our other car, which was housed in our Braselton, Georgia, shop, about fifty-five miles north of Atlanta. Something similar happened to us in 2019 and we wound up not racing because of the complicated logistics. This year we thought we had corrected everything but apparently not.

Two of our crewmembers volunteered to make the trip back to Braselton, and one of our other crew drove them to the Orlando airport (about two hours away). Since one of the two guys was from Braselton, he had a car at the Atlanta airport, which gave them a way to get to our shop. They arrived at the shop late that afternoon, loaded the car into a trailer we had there, and towed it back to Sebring, arriving at about 2:15 a.m.—a ten-hour trip after having worked since 6 a.m. that morning. They were back at the track again at 6 a.m. Then they began the preparations for the car and we took it out in an early test session.

Racing this car put us in a higher class than we wanted, in terms of competing for a championship, since champion points are accumulated by your finishing position plus the number of cars you beat in your class. The higher class is somewhat more competitive, so the opportunity to achieve a better finishing position was more difficult. We nonetheless pushed onward.

This series is a three-race format: two sprint races with a single driver and one endurance race with two drivers. In the first sprint race, I finished in sixth place and in the second sprint race I finished fourth. Not what I wanted, but I finished ahead of one guy who had finished third in the 2020 championship when I won, so I was good. Also, I knew we would do better in the endurance race the next day. Hugh and I usually do well when driving together and we took comfort in potentially winning the endurance race, as we have in the past.

I started the endurance race and was holding my own until lap four. That's when the car gave me an ABS sensor warning. ABS is the system that keeps the brakes from locking up under extreme pressure. Then the next lap I was going into Turn 7, which is a high-speed braking area, and the left front tire locked up and flat spotted that tire.* This should not have happened for two reasons: 1) the ABS is supposed to prevent it, and 2) I was turning to the right so the outside tire—the left front—should have been loaded with weight and should not have locked up. But it did.

As expected, the car then had a huge vibration. I was just hanging on, driving slowly and not as aggressively as usual. While I didn't lose any positions, I didn't make up any ground either. I was just waiting until Hugh started driving after the pit crew had given him new tires—then we'd show them.

---

* Whenever the brakes lock up on any car it can create a flat spot on a portion of the tire. This is referred to as *flat spotting*. As that flat spot rotates it creates a vibration. Also, once a tire is flat spotted, whenever you hit the brakes hard it will have a tendency to come to that same spot, which will make the flat spot worse and wear the tire through the cords. Then the tire blows out.

When we made the stop, Hugh got tires and fuel and took off after the leaders. He was out about three laps when one of the other cars dumped oil over most of the track. These double yellow periods behind the safety car usually last a few laps, but this one was different. The car that dumped the oil did so over so much of the track that the yellow was *extremely* long. How long? It lasted most of the rest of the race and Hugh only had one lap to make up positions when the flag went green again. So we finished P4, which was as good as we could do with so little time to really race. We would have won if we had those laps. This is the "shoulda, coulda, woulda" part of racing.

We did manage to get some points. The prior year we tallied zero points for the Sebring race since we didn't race at all—and we still won the championship. Another bonus was the absence of damage to our car.

In reflecting on the weekend, I was disappointed about not getting more points, particularly after such a great outing at Daytona in December 2020 with a P2 and three P1s in the sprint races, then a P1 in the enduro and winning the championship to boot. I was disappointed about not winning the endurance race since Hugh and I win most of them. When I mentioned this to Hugh, he responded, "Not a bad weekend. They all can't be total successes—nobody else would bother to show up." He's right.

The message here is that we really never know what is going to happen. We do our best to plan and have things correct before an event, but you never really know what's going to happen until things start . . . happening.

In a crude way, this is part of what makes racing exciting. Life is a lot like that too. You never know how it's going to turn out until you start living it. And once you start, you have to live it all the way until the end to truly experience it and find out what happens. Of course, there will be testing moments, but we need to look at things with a positive attitude. It's the surprises that make it interesting.

In the movie *Forrest Gump*, Forrest had a conversation with his mother about life when she mentioned that "life is like a box of chocolates. You never know what you're going to get." Then, Forrest questioned her about surprises and she responded, "at the carnival there is the unpredictability of the roller coaster and predictability of the Ferris wheel" and after a brief pause his mother said, "I always liked the roller coaster best." And that's the way life is.

A story told by Mike Vance in one of the CDs in his "Creative Leadership System" collection takes this can-do thinking in unknown environments a step further. It's an example of how to flip the script from dealing with unknowns to creating as many knowns as possible.

Walt Disney had built Disneyland in California, but he realized that he was hamstrung to make his real vision possible. The company only controlled what was within the perimeter of the amusement park itself. They had no say over the roads, hotels, and eating establishments that popped up across the street and lessened the vibe they wanted their customers to experience when they entered the park. When Walt and the company leaders began to envision the Disney World concept in Florida, they wanted to have control of everything possible.

At the time, they had been acquiring land through shell companies so as not to alert others as to what was occurring—they didn't want to drive up the land prices. Walt engaged a legal team to evaluate and review the concept of how best to control their environment. The legal team came back and said it can't be done. After some time passed, Walt engaged a second legal team, which came back with the same answer: it couldn't be done.

Then Walt engaged a third law firm, which said the only way to achieve what he wanted was to make Disney World a municipality under the law. When Walt asked how he could do that, the answer was that the State of Florida's constitution would need to change. A little while passed before there was Walt Disney on television, explaining why Florida's citizens should vote to support a measure on the ballot to change the state's constitution.

The lesson here is you can have a dream, but to make it come true you need to stick with your vision. Understand that you may need to have the appropriate capital to be able to get it, that it may take time, and that you may need to adjust or recalibrate your vision to make it possible, but it is possible if you are tenacious. There may be errors or setbacks along the way and you may need to make sacrifices along the way. Some are worth it; others are not. The question is whether you're really willing to make them.

26

Think Before You Quit

"Many of life's failures are people who did not realize how close they were to success when they gave up."

Thomas Edison

As I've mentioned previously, in racing we do a lot of planning. We plan for the race, for preparation of the cars, transportation of the cars and equipment, a race strategy, a strategy for the start, etc. However, sometimes instead of a specific plan we have only a general vision or target. We need to be deliberate in thinking through things and in making changes in plans, but sometimes we just need to wing it. However, as we work through the plan and its various steps, we need to have enough confidence in our planning that we don't get easily discouraged. Doubt can lead us to change things precipitously.

During driver development, we create a process that is tailored to each individual and his or her stage of development. The various steps are constantly evaluated so that they represent a progression of that individual, with the ultimate objective of becoming a better driver. To that end, we need to have confidence in the plan and in the designer of the plan (usually a professional co-driver) and not give up on the plan too soon. Giving up too soon is where most folks fail.

Working through the racing program and working to get to a given result made me think about a time several years ago when I was in consulting. I was doing a project in Sacramento with a colleague of mine, Jim. We were staying at a hotel near the state capitol building in the middle of town. It was wintertime so it was pretty dark by dinner.

We asked each other where we should go to eat. Because we were new to the city, we decided to go the highway route and just drive in the general direction of where we thought there would be restaurants. During our drive, Jim suggested a restaurant, and he found the street on a map we had in the rental car. The route we took was highway and the map we had indicated we should keep going in the same direction. So we did.

Once we exited, the roads became more like city roads and then eventually a road with a cobblestone surface with railroad tracks in it. The neighborhood was industrial and had lots of barking junkyard dogs behind fences, which we guessed were for security. We became very concerned with the industrial nature of the neighborhood, so much so that we discussed whether we should even go to the restaurant. We convinced ourselves that we should abandon this restaurant and go somewhere else, which we did. So we turned around and headed back in the direction from which we had come. We spotted a chain restaurant, had dinner there, and made it back to the hotel for the evening.

The next day, we finished work early and decided to have Mexican food, so we asked the hotel clerk where to go. He suggested a place not far from the hotel. Since the hotel clerk suggested it we figured we'd be okay, and we wanted Mexican food since we were in California. The clerk said the place was about four blocks away, so we decided to walk, since it was still light out.

We started walking down the street on which the hotel was located. After about two blocks, we found we were walking on the sidewalk of a cobblestone street. As we continued walking, we started to realize that this was the very same roadway we had been on the previous night, heading to the other restaurant. We came upon the Mexican restaurant we were headed to and just a little further up the street, maybe three or four doors, was the restaurant we were headed to the evening before. As it turned out, we were only a few blocks away from the previous evening's restaurant. More importantly, when we turned around and drove the twenty minutes back, we were actually only four blocks away from the hotel. Because it was dark, we never realized how close we were to the restaurant or the hotel.

What does this have to do with racing or life? A lot.

Many times when we are focused on meeting a goal, we never look up to see where we are. Perhaps because we are so focused, we lose perspective. We might have tunnel vision in which we lose our bearings and our peripheral awareness. Sometimes having a partner can assist here.

But in this example, both of us were too distracted—by the need to eat, or to get back to the hotel to get to bed, or the darkness, or the unfamiliar turf, or the unfamiliar environment.

Whatever it was, it caused us to lose perspective and we simply gave up on the objective too soon.

This often happens to us in racing, in business, or in life. We need to pursue our goals but also need to be reflective and not allow our focus or goal-directedness to overpower our ability to maintain perspective. If we just slow things down a little, and don't pressure ourselves too much, things may come to us.

27

Teammates, Bonding, and Shared Goals

"Character is simply habit long continued."

Plutarch

I severed my Achilles tendon while racing at Canadian Tire Motorsports Park in 2017. Even after having my tendon repaired, I was not racing. In fact, I couldn't even drive a streetcar because the severed tendon was in my right leg and after having surgery I had a cast (and then a boot) up to my knee. Team members needed to wheel me in a wheelchair through the airports so that I wouldn't slow them down getting to the plane. When exiting planes we used the wheelchair again, more for the efficiency of the team members with whom I was traveling. I wanted to support my teammates; attending the races was the most direct way of doing it. Things didn't really change because I was hurt, other than putting Hugh in the car to drive with Guy.

While many thought that if I couldn't drive racing would just stop, my injury actually brought our team closer. There was a bigger plan for TGM to evolve into a great professional race team, become a player in the racing world, and garner sponsorship monies. Stopping was not an option. A certain bond develops among teammates. You become closer—almost like family. That bond creates a closeness and caring for one another. The bond strengthens in the face of adversity, like an injury, because everyone cares for each other.

The next race was about three weeks after my surgery and we were racing at Road America in Elkhart Lake, Wisconsin. This was to be a good track for us, and Hugh and Guy were expected to do well. They were also like mother hens to me, always following me around and wondering if I needed anything. I mention this because before the race, a rainstorm pelted us. Everything was totally soaked. Not a pleasant experience being outside. We were fortunate to have the hauler and to have erected the canopy before the rain got really heavy.

We used golf carts to go everywhere, since they could help prevent us from getting soaked. At one point, Hugh and Guy drove me to the bathroom. I was on crutches and the bathroom floor was totally soaked and kind of slippery. Water everywhere. I carefully entered the bathroom and Hugh was following me closely, worried that I was going to fall. I waited patiently for a urinal located next to a wall because I needed to rest against it with my left side and not use my left crutch.

So here I am, leaning against the wall with my left shoulder, left crutch still under my left arm, in rain gear, trying to keep dry.

This allowed me to use my right hand to do my business while I still had my right crutch under my right arm. At this time Hugh is in the bathroom, as well, strategically located about three urinals to my right. He's cautiously doing his business while at the same time watching that I wouldn't fall. So far, so good.

But as I moved my right arm while doing my business, my right crutch slips out to the right side because of the wet floor. I'm still braced against the wall on my left side, so it's just the crutch that slips, but Hugh looks over and thinks I'm going to fall. What happens instead is the rubber crutch pad (the one that looks like a hot dog bun) on top of my right crutch gets caught on my rain jacket and comes off. The rubber pad does a few back flips in the air, rotates a few turns, and plummets into a urinal. Hugh is looking at this in disbelief, now confident that I'm not going to fall. He's staring at the crutch pad in the urinal. He knows I'm immobile and he's worried that if I bend over I'm going to fall.

"I guess I gotta get it for you," he says. He plucks it out of the urinal and we both go over to the sinks to wash our hands—and to rinse off the crutch pad.

The purpose of this little story is to illustrate the bonds that evolve between teammates. They're like the bonds that evolve between soldiers in battle. It's the reliance on one another, the respect for one another, and the ability to help each other out regardless of the situation. Teammates understand this, but others don't—and likely never will.

I currently have three co-drivers and we each have a bond. We help each other and trust each other and we are secure in knowing we have each other's backs. If you don't have teammates like this, you don't really have a team. A team is not simply a group of individuals with multiple individual interests or goals that just so happen to wear the same uniform. No, teammates share a common goal and they work together to achieve that goal. This is the only way to achieve success as a team.

28

Getting to "We": Having a Teammate or Partner

"The thing that I've learned is that there is no 'them.' This is what everybody does: make a distinction about 'them.' It's just us."

Ken Burns

There are many individuals on a team. But high performing teams have dedicated team members—that's what makes them winners. (This is particularly true of professional race teams.) Great team members may have egos, but they are also excellent at their individual positions. This excellence is what makes their team great. The key is to have a team of individuals function as a unit to achieve great results, as opposed to the team being simply the sum of individual performances. As the saying goes, "the whole is greater than the sum of its parts."

In racing, this applies to the mechanics, the tire guys, the fuel guys, and everyone else. It also applies to the drivers. In endurance racing, drivers typically share a car and their combined performance dictates how high in the standings the team finishes. The car has handling characteristics, but drivers may have their own preferences about how they want the car to handle. Complications arise when these preferences collide and what works for one driver doesn't work for another. One driver could be turning in very fast lap times and wind up in the lead. But when he hands the car off, the next driver's performance is much worse. This can and does happen.

One driver will often demand things that disadvantage his team's other drivers. You see this in professional racing, where there is competition for driver positions and there can be pay variance between teammates. The better the performance among a team's professional drivers, the better will be that driver's relative position for retaining his position on that team and/or getting offers to drive for another team in a larger series for more money. What evolves is a competition not only between teams, but also among drivers on the same team (often in the same car) who are supposedly working to achieve the same goal.

Said differently, initially there are two "me's" as individual drivers. But when the two "me's" are combined, the result can be one great performer and another poor performer. As individuals, they may achieve an acceptable performance. However, if they can work together to accommodate the high performer and facilitate a better relative performance by the lower performer, "we" is being realized.

What's needed is a reconciliation of sorts between the two drivers to overcome each driver making his own decision without thinking about the impact on the other. These are generally "win-lose" scenarios. It works for one but not the other.

The problem can be caused by egos, competition, or the need for some type of dominance of one over the other. Failing to identify the cause of the conflict, and failing to resolve it, will ultimately result in a failure of the pairing—be they drivers or partners in other aspects of life, including life partners. The solution generally depends on dropping the egos or the need for dominance. Sometimes the conflicts stem from someone being immature or lacking self-confidence. If this can be identified, it's much easier to resolve the problem.

Once we recognize that the conflict begins with a failure to communicate, a resolution is possible. Accordingly, we need to communicate. Many marriages and other relationships face the same challenges. In these situations, the more communication, the better. And never assume the other party already recognizes the problem—or won't care about it.

When it comes to racing, communicate about the car, performance, what data you need, etc. Both drivers need to be on the same page and understand that their collective performance will be what gets them to the top of the leader board, which is the objective.

While writing this book, I reflected on what my co-drivers have taught me since we started racing together in 2013, through to today. While I learned many things from all of our co-drivers, here I list the single most important things I have learned and why they've been important. I have learned and why they've been important. You should notice the progressivity and that I kept learning, which is, after all, the most important thing in life.

David Murry – it's about weight management

David was my first professional co-driver. These pros know more and different things about being fast than most amateur instructors. That's because the amateur instructors want to get on the track and be safe but not necessarily fast. Being fast means taking on some risk, which may not work out. Amateur racing is about being safe and having fun.

 David taught me that driving a car fast is primarily about weight management—perceiving and feeling how the weight is positioned on the car's four wheels and feeling how the weight moves with the application of the steering, throttle, and brakes. This was critical for me.

Guy Cosmo – charge every corner

Guy taught me to look at each corner as a challenge and to charge every one. If you make a mistake on a corner, put that behind you as soon as possible and move on to the next corner immediately. In this manner, you are always looking and moving forward.

Hugh Plumb – induce understeer

Understeer is the tendency of the car not to want to turn. When in a corner, we tend to be overly concerned about what will happen if we turn the steering wheel too much. We need to get comfortable with inducing understeer and turning the wheel more. Hugh taught me to "induce understeer." In the end, the car will slow down and eventually turn. At that point we need to start managing the car's turn and shift our focus to the exit.

Matt Plumb – corner entry speed

Matt pushed me to enter corners faster and to learn how to manage the car's speed with additional steering inputs. Turning the wheel will induce a little understeer, which will slow the car or scrub off speed. We do not need to or want to use the brakes as that will shift too much weight to the front of the car, which will intensify the understeer—the exact opposite of what we want it to do in the corner.

Owen Trinkler – exit speed is the key

Owen taught me that a key to a fast lap time is exit speed. The goal is to get the car pointed in the right direction and then get back to full throttle—and hold it—as soon as possible. When I am approaching the apex of the corner, I want to have made my transition from brake to throttle and have begun the progressive throttle application. My target is to get back to full throttle by the apex of the turn.

Mark Hamilton Peters (MHP) – turn twice

When entering a corner, how much wheel (steering input) I use depends on the tightness of the corner. However, MHP instructed me not to merely maintain static steering input for the entire turn but to induce a little more steering input when in the middle of the corner. This will tend to get the car pointed toward the exit in a straighter line and allow you to get to full throttle for the exit, thereby increasing exit speed.

This learning happened in a progressive manner over a nine-year period. I think the lessons should be adopted one at a time —not all at once—and perhaps with some assistance from a pro. The result will be progressive learning that builds on itself—just as in everyday life.

29

Givers and Takers

"Two things define you: Your patience when you have nothing and your attitude when you have everything."

George Bernard Shaw

"My father said there are two kinds of people in the world:
givers and takers. The takers may eat better, but the givers
sleep better."

Marlo Thomas

The racing world has all kinds of people. I am referring to
"attitudes."

Some folks will help you and others will not. Yet others may
intentionally tell you things that get you headed in the wrong
direction. Some professional drivers come at racing with a sense
of entitlement. They believe they are entitled to get past you or to

be in front of you and the sooner you agree with that the better off you'll be. We don't know why this is, but it just is.

This all boils down to two types—*givers* and *takers*. We can all spot them. In racing, I have encountered folks who have helped me immensely, yet others have hindered me. This can play out both off the track and on it. There's an unwritten rule that two competitors can work together, with one staying behind the other for most of the race. But the "gloves come off" in the last few laps as they race each other for position.

Generally, racers like to help one another. In this sense, they are *givers*. However, they only help one another up until the point where that help might make you faster than them. Then the help stops.

Takers only see their own angle. They want what they want and that's all that matters. They can allow you to believe they are helping you, but they really are only seeing their own interests.

Takers fail to understand that folks see them for what they are. That means others will not want to help them when they need something, whether on the track or off.

I once worked with a health care executive who was a bigwig, but he was widely known as a taker. He would not share information or techniques with others in similar capacities, even though those others shared information with him. When he found himself out of a job, the other executives in similar positions would not help him find another position. When I asked the others to help, they said he was a taker and refused. It was a powerful reminder of the old saying, "what goes around comes around."

30

Dealing with Pressure, Uncertainty, and Surprise

"He who is not every day conquering some fear has not learned the secret of life."

Ralph Waldo Emerson

In 2018, I was racing in the Ferrari Challenge. My teammates and I decided to enter the world finals in Italy, which were being held at the world-famous Monza racecourse. We raced there and had two podium finishes (P3 and P2). At the World Finals, all the Ferrari Challenge drivers from around the world race together. It includes a series of races that are initially separate: the North American drivers, the European drivers, and the Asian drivers each race in their own groups. There is also a common race where drivers from each group all race against one another, based on their race class. It's a big deal in the Ferrari world.

Once that race was over, Hugh asked if I wanted to enter a race that was bigger than our current IMSA series races. After thinking about it, I told him maybe we should race at Le Mans in France (the biggest sportscar race in the world). We then developed a strategy to race there, perhaps in 2020. The plan included talking to race teams from Porsche and from Ferrari. We believed that these were the only two manufacturers who understood the complicated politics of Le Mans.

We held those talks and moved ahead with other parts of our plan in 2019. We even set up a test drive of a Ferrari GT3 car at the Indianapolis Motor Speedway in 2019, because it looked as if we were going the Ferrari route. We were planning to enter an event called the Road to Le Mans, which would make us eligible to participate in the real Le Mans race. The racecourse at Le Mans is only available once per year because it uses public roads; I would be racing on a track where I had never driven. This put us on a multi-year schedule. We even scheduled a trip to Europe so we could drive a Ferrari GT3 on a few other tracks.

In January 2020, I raced in the IMSA Michelin Pilot Series in Chevrolet Camaros and decided to stay over for the 24 Hours of Daytona. I had the privilege of watching from the Cadillac Suite, which was a great experience. At some point late in the night, while watching the cars race, the thought occurred to me—why don't I drive in this race instead of Le Mans? I knew the track, I had access to it for practice, and I had co-drivers who had driven in the race previously. It made sense, so I shared the idea with Hugh. He agreed that it made a lot of sense. And that's the origin of the idea of racing in the 24 Hours of Daytona, which we did in January 2021.

Shortly after this, the COVID-19 pandemic hit and Team TGM decided to cease its primary race focus while I turned my attention to research and the new virus. However, the thought of the 24 Hours of Daytona still lingered.

In mid-2020, Hugh asked if I was still interested in running the 24 Hours of Daytona. When I said yes, he responded, "Well, we'd better start planning." And we did.

We developed a plan, purchased a car, and cultivated a working relationship with another team to run the car for us. That team had many years of experience in this race, with the car we had decided to purchase—a Porsche GT3 R. I have a lot more experience with the Porsche platform than the Ferrari platform, so going with Porsche made a lot of sense.

We did extensive testing and preparation so we would be all set for the race. At the time, it was the biggest race I had ever participated in. It includes the best prototype and GT drivers from around the world, as well as the best drivers in the United States. There were drivers from IndyCar, NASCAR, and IMSA, as well as some famous drivers from Europe. A first-class field of very fast cars and highly accomplished drivers.

And then there was me. I went through various mental contortions, from "I can do this" to "Why did I think of this?" to "Can I do this?" and back to "I can do this." In that order.

One difference between the cars used in Daytona and our regular cars is the degree of sophistication. For example, the car has a back-up camera for a rear view and the camera has a built-in radar, which monitors up to forty objects simultaneously and indicates the top four threats. The approaching cars are measured based on relative speeds, so the system tells you the closing rate and when it spots the top four. When cars are going to pass you, it tells you which side. There is also a spotter, who communicates with the driver via radio about the position of cars in the same class as well as other approaching cars. The spotter will also tell us when cars are three wide and the class of those cars. In other words, lots and lots of information, which gets delivered while you're moving at 170–180 mph and monitoring everything that's going on with the car. I became very reliant on the spotter, particularly for information at night.

The team decided I would start the race and do so from the back, since that was safest. As they say, "in order to finish first, you must first finish." (Even the most accomplished racers have often been known to be too enthusiastic on the start.) Each driver's stint in the car was to run about 55–58 minutes.

The start went well and I held pace. When I returned to driving a few hours later, the sky was dark. And there was a glitch. The spotter did not have power up at his station, so I did not have access to his information, which I was now trained to rely on. I told myself not to worry as I still had my mirrors and the rear camera. A few laps after that I was exiting Turn 6—a lefthander which leads back onto the banking—and a prototype (a single seat, purpose-built, very fast racecar that has a swoopy body and doesn't look anything like a streetcar) hip checked my left front side, slightly knocking me into the wall on my right side. This was not a big deal, except that it rendered my right-side mirror unusable. But I stayed calm, reminding myself not to worry and just deal with it.

At this point I had no spotter and no right mirror, I was alone in the car, there was no one to help me, and I was in the biggest race of my career, with some of the best drivers in the world. No pressure, huh? I just dealt with it.

This was part of my evolution as a professional driver. Earlier on, these challenges would have bothered me and I might have panicked. Instead, I just radioed in and went on and dealt with what I had, making an assessment as to what I had available and what I needed to do to adapt.

Here's another life lesson. The unexpected often occurs. You probably don't want it to, and perhaps it shouldn't. But it does. Sometimes there are multiple occurrences simultaneously. In such situations, you merely need to reassess and figure what you have and how to use it in your present situation.

In the race situation I described above, I radioed in about the mirror—but more for my teammates who would follow. Maybe the team could see it as I went by or on television monitors. Or maybe the team could plan to fix it during the next pit stop. But for me it was what it was and I couldn't do anything to immediately remedy it. As someone once told me, "Things that happen to you are neither good things or bad things. It's all in how *you* look at them." Maybe this was one of those situations.

31

Perspective: Knowing Where You Are in the Grand Scheme

"Success is to be measured not so much by the position that one has reached in life as by the obstacles he has overcome."

Booker T. Washington

"The measure of success is not how much you have but how far you've come from where you started."

Ted Giovanis

I used to run a lot, particularly before I switched to racing cars in my mid-30s. The two activities are fundamentally different, but they have one key parallel: there are always people ahead of you—and there are destined to be people behind you. Progress is about moving up the ladder one rung at a time. And that progress is going to be realized by focusing on how you can improve—and not by focusing on what other people are doing. You can't control their speed, so it only makes sense to focus on yourself. The rest will take care of itself.

Runners have a certain rhythm or cadence to their pace. It's more difficult to run at another person's rate or pace because when you run slower, your rhythm is off and you use more energy. I was part of a running group and I would rotate among the guys of differing paces depending the training day we were on—hard or recovery, and varied by length of the run.

I used to run with a guy—Dick, who was much faster than me. We ran together on his "recovery" day—the day after he had a hard run. I would run with some of my work colleagues on my recovery days, so I could run at their pace, which was slower than my race pace but still was hard for them. I was running about 70 miles per week and, in running terms, I was in pretty good shape.

In 1983, I took a job at a large health system in Cumberland, Maryland. Cumberland is in the mountains of western Maryland. I was able to run every day at lunch and would vary my runs from easy to hard. Cumberland has tons of hills and I learned that I needed to know my route in advance, because otherwise I could be in for an unpleasant surprise.

I was running 5 miles fast one day, then 10 miles of hills, then recover with runs of 6–7 miles. On the weekend, I would run with another guy, Tommy, who worked for the local newspaper. Tommy was always training for a marathon (which is 26.2 miles), so every Saturday I would do a 15–17 mile run with him at his pace. Then I would recover on Sundays with a 7–8 mile run.

Needless to say, I was in the best running shape of my life. I was 134 pounds—"lean and mean," as they say.

I was running races too. Running became a way for me to meet my competitive urges, since I had given up racing cars temporarily, having found running. And it turned out that I was pretty good at running, despite having taken it up at the ripe old age of thirty-three. I was flying high, so to speak.

It was around this time that Baltimore's city government was building an underground subway. The local roadrunners groups started what they called the Great Subway Race, which traced the subway's layout for 8 miles. The race started at a mall on the western side of Baltimore and ended at the inner harbor. While there were a few small inclines, they weren't really hills, and the overall course involved running down grades, not up them. In Cumberland, there were bigger hills along the fitness courses in the parks.

I signed up for the race and because I was alone I waited on the sideline at the start, just behind the seeded runners (the fast guys). When the gun went off to start the race, I jumped in behind the seeded group and ran at my own pace. As I approached the halfway point, I was right about on the fastest four-mile pace I had ever run.

I was feeling proud of myself, when I heard someone say, "Hey Ted." I looked to the left and saw Dick, who I had run with when I worked in Baltimore. "Can I run with you?" he asked. "Sure," I responded.

(Dick was guy I ran with on his recovery days because he was faster, but I did not focus on that during this race.)

So Dick and I ran the rest of the race together and about a half-mile from the end we passed the first-place woman, who had recently won the Maryland Marathon. Given her speed, I was feeling pretty good about passing her. As we approached the final turn, we were beside the Baltimore Civic Center and about to sprint for the chute to the finish line.

"Come on Dick, let's go" I said.

"I'm not going through the chute," he replied.

After the race we were talking briefly, and since I hadn't seen him in a while, I suggested we hang out, to which he responded, "I can't. I gotta run back and get my car."

So here I am having just run the fastest 8 miles of my career, I beat the first-place woman, and Dick is on a 16-mile training run—at my pace all the way.

To reinforce what I said at the start of the chapter, in running, racing, and so many other endeavors, it's always a "me" versus "me" scenario. I have found that if I focus on me versus me, the me versus the other guy takes care of itself. It can be useful to do comparatives to others to figure out how "you" can improve. But always comparing yourself to others leads to frustration and may lead to unreasonable goals. I have told my children that there will always be folks who have more and others who have less. So don't worry about that. Just focus on yourself and you will be better off than when you started.

32

Management and Leadership: Learning from Mike Vance

"... and suddenly I realized that I was no longer driving the car consciously, I was driving it by a kind of instinct, only I was in a different dimension."

Ayrton Senna

"Treat people as if they were what they ought to be and you help them to become what they are capable of being."

Johann Wolfgang Von Goethe

When I was moving through the management ranks, I looked to several individuals for inspiration and leadership. One of those individuals was Mike Vance, whom I have referenced throughout this book. While I did not work with or for Mike, his teachings and talks helped me evolve in my thinking and become what I am today. I have listened to his talks on leadership and creativity and they have helped me in different parts of my life. His ideas have become ingrained in my thinking and they have shaped much of the substance in this book.

He liked to illustrate his ideas by drawing comparisons to Star Wars. A prime example: he talked a lot about the Force.

Mike said there are three management philosophies, approaches, or positions:

The first approach is embodied in "I am the Force," which refers to the manager asserting that he (or she) is, well…the Force. In other words, a dictator.

The second approach is "I have the Force." It amounts to, "if you're good, I'll give you a piece of it." This is a benevolent dictator. He or she will still be a son of a bitch, but still wants to be liked.

His third approach referred to an emerging style utilized by successful leaders. "YOU have the Force." This suggests that "if you allow me, I will help you develop your Force so that you can maximize it."

The third approach is focused on individuals. It recognizes their values, drive, and motivation and helps channel it. I have used the concepts above in my work in health care finance and now in the TGM race team and the Jayne Koskinas Ted Giovanis Foundation. I want to create a provocative environment where folks can feel free to express their ideas and creativity and can pursue their work with their innate and acquired talents. This ultimately leads to more progress, as well as more fulfillment for those involved.

Remember, "YOU have the Force."

In his seminars on Creative Leadership and Creative Thinking, Mike discussed what he called the Four Levels of Competence. What follows is a paraphrase of the seminars.

You can perceive these levels as a hierarchy. Employees or team members can evolve through the different levels. And the levels can be used to gauge individuals you encounter in the work environment and throughout life. Sometimes people do not evolve, but you need to know where they are in order to measure their performance and decide if they need to be removed from the team or workforce. This can be on a race team or in a business.

UNCONSCIOUS INCOMPETENCE

The first level is for individuals who are incompetent but don't know it. They are not suited for their position and consistently underperform. It's going to be difficult for these people to evolve upward because they typically don't understand they are poor performers and there might not be anyone to tell them they are incompetent. But even if told, they might not be able to recognize their incompetence and thus would not be able to improve. Perhaps if these individuals could comprehend their incompetence, they could evolve. But who should tell them and how is always a dilemma. While we want to believe they can improve, it's possible they can't.

CONSCIOUS INCOMPETENCE

The next level up is Conscious Incompetence. Individuals at this level know they are incompetent but they try to fly below the radar. They seem to be comfortable with their incompetence and don't want to do anything about it. They are also clever enough to take the steps necessary to hide. If they devoted as much energy to improving as they did to hiding, they could improve. We have all encountered folks in this level and it's difficult to get them to focus on improving their performance.

CONSCIOUS COMPETENCE

This level includes folks who know they are good (but not great) and they know exactly why they are good. Perhaps it's their training or their drive or other qualities. These folks can be helpful to an organization or team because they can help train others to enhance their performance and therefore raise the organization's total level of performance. Their issue is evolving to the next level—to be great. This can be difficult as there's no real process to follow to achieve greatness. But one of the keys is to be able to engage in self-criticism while participating in an activity, while also being open to constructive criticism from others, because people who own up to shortcomings or mistakes are well positioned to fix them. People who can't admit to having any shortcomings are never going to get better.

UNCONSCIOUS COMPETENCE

This level is composed of individuals who understand they are competent but they do not know exactly what makes them great at what they do. For example, a professional running back might be great, but because elements of his greatness are instinctual he doesn't understand how difficult it is for mere mortals to look left but run to the right. Similarly, it's like a race driver who knows to turn in at a certain point but when they rise to the next level, they just know what to do. It's like comparing the brushstrokes of an artist to someone who is painting by numbers.

Evolution through the various levels enables individuals to be categorized within any organization or team. It also means we can evaluate them at their levels to see if they have the potential to evolve.

33

Air Wakes: Being Cognizant of the Effects of What We Do

"The most important single ingredient in the formula for success is knowing how to get along with people."

Theodore Roosevelt

"A kind heart is a fountain of gladness, making everything in its vicinity freshen into smiles."

Washington Irving

In racing, we need to be cognizant of the actions we take and the impact of these actions on ourselves and others. This was brought home to me one day when I was testing cars at Virginia International Raceway.

I was driving my Porsche GT3 Cup car, which has about 460 horsepower but weighs about 2,650 pounds. It's considered a fast car, even in the world of racing. It also has a lot of down force. As I have explained previously, down force is the rough equivalent of adding weight to your car without actually doing so. With down force, you're pressing the car closer to the ground, through engineering design and aerodynamics. The effect enables you to go faster through the corners. However, a high down force car, once it gets to speed on the straightaway, creates a lot of turbulence around and in back of itself. This is known as an air wake.

While at VIR, I was on-track with someone in a Porsche 914. Its motor is in the rear and there's not much to the car up front. The result is little down force and no weight up front, which means the car can be a little skittish.

While on the back straight at VIR, I was coming up on the 914 doing about 140–150 mph. I was staying in the car's draft (the wake he was making once his car made a hole in the air) to maximize my speed. I pulled out to pass and I stayed about a foot off his left side to take advantage of the side draft. I zoomed past and then got in front of him so that he could take advantage of my draft (we were just practicing, not racing).

Later, I talked to the driver in the paddock. I asked him if my pass destabilized his car. He said it did. I told him I needed to recognize that other cars do not have the same down force and stability as my car. I apologized for being so close and said I would give him a little more space between our cars next time. (The space allows the air turbulence to settle a bit so it's not as disruptive to the other cars.)

What does this tell us about life? Virtually everything we do has consequences. We may not know they're there, or what they are, but there are ripple effects. They can be direct trade-offs, like in spending money for something. For example, you could commit to a mortgage or other debt and fail to recognize the longer-term ramifications related to that commitment, such as having less money for something else. This can apply to governments too. They can make commitments and not realize the long-term effects.

All of our actions create a wake, and sometimes we need to take other actions to offset that wake. The effects of our wake may not only affect others but us as well.

34

Look for Small Achievements and Applaud Them

"Though we crave certainty for almost everything, innovation and progress happen when we allow ourselves to embrace uncertainty."

Simon Sinek

"Imagination was given to man to compensate for what he isn't. A sense of humor was provided to console him for what he is."

Horace Walpole

It was 2013. We had recently reconstituted the TGM racing program. We revamped the program and brought on a professional driver named David. He was an experienced pro and had driven many international and national tracks, including Le

Mans. We could learn a lot from him, and we did. Because he was a pro, his lap times were always faster than mine. However, the plan and the process were to get me to drive more like a pro.

We were racing at Road Atlanta, which we considered our home track since we have a race shop directly adjacent to it. We were racing our new BMW 330, which has a six-speed manual transmission. There was heavy rain, which was expected to continue the entire time we were there. Road Atlanta is a fast track and has a lot of elevation changes. Because of the steep grades, there is considerable water runoff in many places. The water runs down the hills and it eventually needs to cross the track's lowest spot. There was water running across the track in several key places: at the bottom of the S turns and across the middle of the back straight, which is a high-speed area where our car would be in fifth or sixth gear.

I had never raced on this track in the rain so there was much to learn. Nevertheless, we were hopeful we would place well. We figured that the rain would be a great equalizer because the more powerful cars have traction issues when the track is wet.

But this is not quite how it turned out. Several teams, though not ours, had crashes during the practice sessions. It was treacherous on the track, particularly if you hit the water and had not approached it from the correct angle. A wet track forces you to change your driving and go to different parts of the track than you would in the dry. Also, in the areas where the water runs across the track, you need to change your line even more to ensure you cross the water streams perpendicularly, which helps prevent hydroplaning.

There was only one issue we encountered that weekend—the defroster blower broke and we could not get a replacement in time for the race. Our workaround was to use a squeegee in the car and attach it to the dashboard with a broom clip—the ones you use in your closet to hold the brooms and mop. We also put heavy applications of Rain-X anti-fog on the inside of the windshield to prevent fogging. Problem addressed, but not necessarily solved.

Soon after I started the race, heat from the engine and transmission was heavily fogging the windshield. My pit crew radioed and told me to start using the squeegee, which I did. During each lap, I would go down the start-finish straight, and once in fifth gear and clear of the high-speed Turn 12 leading onto the front straight, I would unclip the squeegee, wipe the windshield so I could see, and then quickly clip it back in before going into Turn 1, which is a high-speed fourth-gear turn, then up the hill and down the next, avoiding the large water stream coming across the track from right to left at the bottom. Once clear of that stream upon exiting Turn 5, I would again squeegee the windshield before needing to upshift to fifth gear and put the squeegee back before Turn 6. Once through Turns 6 and 7, I was on the back straight (one mile in length and ideal for high speed), which had a water stream running across it from left to right, about three quarters of the way down and just before a heavy braking area. Once onto that back straight, I needed to wait until I was in fifth gear, which is a longer gear, so I would have time to squeegee the windshield. Once in fifth, I needed to quickly wipe the windshield with the squeegee and then put it back before upshifting to sixth and going across the running water and then getting on the brakes to make the hard left-hand slow turn at the end of the straight. This process continued for my entire stint. It wasn't pleasant, but it was bearable.

I had kept the car safe, which is a major concern when racing in these conditions. When I returned to the pit, I handed over driving duties to David, the pro racer, who was doing great until he dropped the squeegee and it wound up in the right passenger footwell. Because he was belted in and had very limited range of movement, he couldn't pick the squeegee up. That meant he could only peer through the very bottom of the windshield on the left side, as everything else was fogged up. He struggled through. His biggest problem was seeing the apexes of the turns when turning to the right since that part of the windshield was still foggy.

This would be the only race in which my fastest lap time was 1.5 seconds per lap faster than David's. While it was unfortunate that we didn't finish higher, I took some small comfort in driving faster than David and I didn't let him forget it for a while. Needless to say, we fixed the defroster situation right after the race.

One lesson from this episode is to take comfort in small achievements because you never know when the next one will happen.

35

Sometimes You Can Control Things That Do Not Appear to Be Within Your Control

"Do I not destroy my enemies when I make them my friends?"

Abraham Lincoln

In racing it's the pole sitters in each race who control the pace of the start, and they can use that pace to their advantage. They can select the gear that is best for "their" cars' RPM and torque range. This allows them to get a jump on the start. If the other cars are in the incorrect ranges, they are disadvantaged on that particular start. This is the advantage of qualifying on the pole for a given race.

Each car has its own specific gearing, and all cars' gearing is not the same. This is innate in the design of the car. For example, a high-performance car generally has lower gearing (which can consume more fuel) while a different car can have higher gearing, which will conserve fuel. When cars are adapted to being race-cars, these innate factors influence where the car is in the RPM range, which impacts where the car is in the power and torque range for that car. This can influence where a given car will be able to start a race.

We were racing at a small track in Ohio called Nelson Ledges. I had not qualified on the pole so I was on the outside pole. I was vying for the championship that year, which meant I really needed to do well in this race. My dilemma was thinking of ways that I could control the start even though I wasn't the pole sitter. There were two factors in play: the pace of the start and where I would be once I got to the first turn (inside or outside).

One of my friends suggested several options: Regarding pace, he recommended that as we were coming down the back straight and the field was forming, I should slow the pace down—a lot. He said I should do this knowing that the pole sitter couldn't just take off and have the field distributed and be getting a real jump on all the other cars, as the starter would call off the start if that happened.

It sounded like a good idea, so I tried it. I slowed the field down to about 30 mph when the normal pace would have been around 60 mph. The rest of the field seemed to lag with me. I was in second gear, which was my preference when racing against this particular pole sitter, and it gave me more of an advantage. So far, so good.

There was another issue. Once I got to Turn 1, I would be in third gear and likely on the outside of that turn, which is usually dirtier than the inside. As racecars drive on the track, rubber scrubs off the tires. These pieces of rubber accumulate on the surfaces of the track where the cars do not generally run, which is mostly on the outside of the track and off the racing line. As such, the racing line can be dirty and slower with these rubber pieces, and there is less traction as well. That meant I would be going faster and traveling a longer distance. When lining up at the start, the cars are traditionally odd on the inside and even on the outside, based on their qualifying times. Therefore the pole sitter being number one was on the inside and I was on the outside. The odd-placed cars are on the inside following the pole sitter (1, 3, 5, 7, 9, etc.) and the even-placed in order on the outside (2, 4, 6, 8, 10, etc.).

I was worried about the track being dirty and having a lot less grip on the outside. My friend suggested that I go to the drivers of all the even numbered cars and explain to them that I was planning on going through Turn 1 on the outside, and that that would be a moving lane, but I needed their help. On the two parade laps, I needed them to scrub their tires (weaving back and forth and applying the brakes in an effort to heat up our tires) while going through Turn 1 and get a lot of the dirty stuff off the track, so it would be faster for all of us. We lined up and went out of the pits for the parade laps and everyone stuck to the plan. Of course, we never told the inside lane cars, so they didn't realize anything until the race started. The race started and the entire outside lane moved up a lot while going around the outside of Turn 1. In fact, by the time we got to Turn 2 and Turn 3, three of the even numbered cars were already in front of the actual pole sitter. In other words, my plan worked.

In the end, I won the race and the fourth-place qualifier (the car behind me on the start) was second, as we were able to maintain the advantage we had gained at the start.

This scenario can arise in our lives, either at work or in other situations. It can be an "enemy of my enemy is my friend" scenario, or you might just be able to work with someone who has a similar objective and can assist you in achieving what you want to accomplish. It's a reminder that being isolated can deprive you of potential opportunities. Sometimes we need to work with others who we don't expect to work with, even when we may not particularly like those folks or we see them as competitors. It's a question of having common or similar interests. Of course, we need to be able to trust them. In the scenario above, that meant being confident that the drivers in the outside lanes wouldn't tell the drivers in the inside lanes. In the end, most of the first five rows of outside lane cars gained positions by working together to get the advantage. Sure, I gained the most because I won the race, but they benefited too. That's what matters.

36

Dealing with Racing Regulatory Bodies

"It's probably better to have him inside the tent pissing out, than outside the tent pissing in."
Lyndon Baines Johnson (about J. Edgar Hoover)

"Education is the ability to listen to almost anything without losing your temper or your self-confidence."
Robert Frost

"How many legs does a dog have if you call his tail a leg? Four, just saying a tail is a leg doesn't make it a leg!"
Abraham Lincoln

There need to be rules that regulate the races and the cars. This is the responsibility of a race sanctioning body that presides over the races and regulates the cars and driver behavior within a given race series. The sanctioning body develops and implements rules that govern the cars and drivers that participate in any series. While technically different, they operate much like any other regulator. They develop rules, those rules are to be followed by race participants, and then the series implements and presides over the series.

THE CARS

There are a variety of manufacturers that participate in racing series. These manufacturers produce their cars to an international specification that is theoretically equal. However, this is not always the case on a racetrack. A race sanctioning body is desirous of having cars be equal on the racetrack. However, because the cars are built by different manufacturers they are inherently different in their on-track performance. While there is an international specification, the cars are different.

The cars are theoretically balanced across the various manufacturers through a process generally referred to as the Balance of Performance (BOP) process. Through this process the sanctioning body attempts to balance the various manufacturer platforms to be somewhat equal within a range of performance. This is a very complicated process that requires much data from the various cars participating in the race events. Sometimes this process works. At other times it does not and it requires further adjustments to tune things in.

The process requires participation by the manufacturers because they know the cars best. However, generally the series is in charge. Determinations are made by the race series based on data obtained from previous race performances. The data is fed into the process, the output from which is adjustment or no adjustment to a specific car's platform. Endurance racing cars require a wide variety of adjustments. There can be adjustments to reduce or increase power, increase or decrease weight, or to otherwise limit on-track performance. Included are changes to the aerodynamics of the car or adjustments to the car's fuel capacity and how fast the car can be refueled through the changes in a restrictor on the fill tube. As you can see, these changes can be varied and complex, as they affect each car's on-track performance in the race. Speed, fuel burn, and number of pit stops can be impacted by these types of changes.

THE DRIVERS

As mentioned in previous chapters, there are many driver egos in racing. These diverse interests and egos can play out in the race. The sanctioning body has the responsibility to oversee and manage these differences. The conflict is that the series is desirous of good aggressive racing, but it wants fair racing too. How this balance is achieved needs to play out during the race. Therefore, race calls need to be made based on what happens on the track.

IMPACTING THE CAR PROCESS

Basically, this is the responsibility of the manufacturers. Manufacturers interact with race teams, as these teams are the customers of the manufacturers. The manufacturers want their teams to do well against the other teams of different manufacturers. Having input can be challenging. This is a negotiation, but also a diplomatic process. Interaction with the sanctioning body requires a balanced approach.

Likewise, the series needs to balance what it does diplomatically. If they upset a manufacturer (who generally pays an annual fee to be in the series) the manufacturer can focus on a different series. The manufacturers are involved because it makes sense for their business. They want to do well. But the series wants balance. A complicated balancing act to achieve a complicated balance. In the end, all the parties need to be involved and need to understand the nature of the process. No one should get greedy. However, mistakes can be made. When they do, they need to be rectified. Therefore, the series needs to understand and be responsive to changes and correct things promptly if they are incorrect.

RELATIONSHIP TO LIFE

It's easy to see the relationship between race series regulation and our dealings in real life. The operative word is *balance*. Balance in how we relate to others and balance in what we do—no big changes unless we are 100 percent sure they are needed. An incremental approach is generally better. It allows folks to see what is being changed and adjusted incrementally—no big swings. Also important is no surprises. People generally do not like surprises, and this applies to almost anything.

If any action is needed, go incrementally. This also needs to be balanced against the need to adjust things over a short timeframe. However, it is important that whoever needs to do the adjusting recognize that those being impacted by the adjustment need to perceive the adjustment as fair, and they need to understand the adjustment. An open, transparent process including dialogue facilitates this, as well as explanation of the reasoning and the sharing of information, data, and analytics. A lack of transparency will cloud and frustrate whatever is being attempted.

37

There's a Difference Between Reality and Games: Simulator Racing Is *Not* Real Racing

"The years teach much which the days never know."

Ralph Waldo Emerson

The use of race simulators is now all the rage. Many, if not most, drivers are using simulators as part of their training. These devices can be a valuable tool to improve race driving and on-track performance. Simple videos may assist in such improvements, but the simulator can allow us to experience a race rhythm for the turns, braking, and throttle modulation; with some full-motion simulators there are even G-forces. Alternatively, watching race videos can also provide some benefits that are crudely similar to a simulator. The videos can provide a useful comparison to a reference lap with video inputs for brake and throttle modulation. These are all tools for assisting in rhythm and improving. Race driving is a hand-eye motor skill and reflexes endeavor. It also involves reaction time and being quick with your feet. Improving any of these, with whatever tools are available, is a good thing.

However, it's important to remember that simulators are just simulations. They are not reality. There is no risk in using them, as they are nothing more than video games matched to a skill. Hypothetically, in a war game when you are shooting at an opponent and the opponent is shooting back, you are fundamentally trying to outsmart the game's algorithm. But when you are shot and the game ends, you simply push the reset button and begin anew. Race simulators are like this too. You can go faster and faster until such time as you crash. Then you simply hit reset and you're back in the pits and begin again. You try to recalibrate to the algorithm and if you don't get that right and crash again—reset. A major concern is the impact this has on our brains. One can get reckless and the behavior is then reinforced, raising the question: What happens when this gets translated onto the real track? Does it instill bad habits that are not recognized by the brain because there is no real risk? You're not hurt, no crash damage to pay for, no time lost for repairs. How do we create perspective with the use of simulators?

Do simulators work? Absolutely. But what role should they play?

There are real-life examples of famous drivers being beaten in a simulator race by racers who have never driven real racecars. When this occurs, does it mean that the sim racers should be driving and not the real racer? Likely not. More likely is that the simulator racer simply figured out the algorithm or figured out how to change the car's set up in the algorithm to get the car matched to the track in the simulator. The G-forces produced by a true racing car cannot be replicated by a simulator—even a full-motion simulator. And the simulator cannot produce real risk.

If the simulator racer spent tons of time on the simulator, he could understand it in a way the real racer could not. However, the reverse is also true. The real racer has thousands of hours in a real racecar that the simulator racer doesn't and knows infinitely more than the simulator racer when placed in that environment.

Real racers are in the "real" game—life—which brings actual risks and actual consequences. They can feel the car move and shift, right down to the seat of their pants. Their brain provides real feedback based upon multiple senses. They feel the car slide sideways and they gauge grip levels. They know when they have made a mistake and know instinctively and reflexively how to correct it. All of this is absent from the simulator.

If the setup is wrong on the simulator, you crash, often frequently. But if the setup is "right" or is what the algorithm wants, you can be blindingly fast. Guess right or understand how to make changes on the setup and you're good on the simulator. In a racecar, the right setup also leads to being fast. But it must be matched to things like the track, time of day, and ambient temperature. Simulators are somewhat similar. However, the consequences of a miscalculation are very different. In simulators and video games, your brain needs to figure out the algorithm. In real life, it's much more complex because there are so many more variables—plus risk and consequences.

38

Aging while Racing (or Anything, Really)

"Excuses are the rocks where our dreams are crushed."

Tim Fargo

"I do not know anyone who has gotten to the top without hard work. That is the recipe. It will not always get you to the top, but it will get you pretty near."

Margaret Thatcher

"Start by doing what's necessary; then do what's possible; and suddenly you are doing the impossible."

Saint Francis of Assisi

"Of course there are moments that you wonder how long you should be doing it because there are other aspects which are not nice of this lifestyle. But I just love winning."

Ayrton Senna

As we age, it affects everything we are involved in, and racing is no different.

I was forty-six years old when I started racing. I was older than most drivers, but I was not way beyond the average age. As I gained experience, I became faster and faster. I won races and regional amateur championships and I set track records in a particular class that stood for five years. In 2006, I moved from amateur to professional racing but continued to have an amateur team of volunteers and amateur co-drivers. In 2013, I reconstituted the team and started racing with a professional co-driver. We also had a professional crew; this coincided with the team beginning to evolve to the next level.

My professional co-driver changed my thinking about racing and driving fast. Previously, I had focused on managing the application of power, which is always a factor. However, the bigger issue is weight management.

Imagine that you have a size 9 shoe and your feet are side by side. Each shoe is approximately 12 inches long and 4 inches wide. Together, your feet occupy about 96 square inches. The portion of the tire that touches the ground is called the contact patch. The car's entire weight is supported by these four patches. Since these four patches support the entire weight of the car, it means they control what the car does and what happens when the weight shifts among them.

These contact patches can do three things: turn, stop, and accelerate. But they can't do them all at the same time to maximum efficiency because there are limits to the adhesion of the tires. As weight moves among these contact patches, it determines what the car can and will do. Getting to the point where one can feel the weight of the car and its movement allows us to evolve in our approach to car control.

It was only upon learning the preceding that I realized everything I was doing regarding my approach to race driving was wrong. This was the time for a major rethink of my approach. But by this point it was 2013 and I was sixty-eight years old. Hmmm. That meant embarking on a plan to reprogram behavior that was part of my muscle and motor memory stretching back several decades. Not impossible, but not easy either.

We use a lot of data in racing and this can assist us in identifying and selecting where improvements can be made. We create benchmark data from the laps of pro co-drivers and then compare lap times and the accompanying data. We have data for essentially anything we can measure through sensors. This includes (but is not limited to) throttle position, brake pressure, steering angle, vehicle speed, and gear selection.

My race team had three professional co-drivers and one of those co-drivers represented my benchmark. I am constantly striving to achieve better results. Imagine my thoughts when I come into the driver's lounge in our hauler and my benchmark driver is comparing himself to another co-driver, looking for ways to improve. Yes, the benchmark is changing and I need to adapt. I can do this because I am committed to improvement. Will I reach the benchmark? Maybe, maybe not. But I'll be better than I am right now, and that's the objective. My approach to racing and life has always been that it's me versus me. I find that if I focus on the me part, the me versus the other guys generally takes care of itself.

Besides having a commitment to improvement, the aging driver needs to deal with several other factors. A fundamental one is that it's more difficult to stay fit. But aging chronologically does not mean the physiological aspects need to follow exactly the same path. There are three factors that can improve our physiological state: fitness, mental acuity, and diet.

Physical fitness. For the aging individual it is always advisable and appropriate to consult your physician before beginning an exercise program.

I find myself devoting more and more time to staying physically fit as I age. The result of engaging in a physical fitness program is that I feel better and I am qualitatively healthier. I have a physical fitness routine that is tailored to racing. It involves more repetitions using lower weight. It creates a stronger, leaner body mass that can endure the rigors of racing. The goal is to endure racing stints without exhaustion. But the routine I've described in the Appendices can help anyone stay fit and control their weight. These routines are based on body weight exercises that use your own body's weight as the resistance. Again, anyone can start here.

Other tools for exercise are also relatively inexpensive and easy to come by. They include dumbbells, weight plates, kettle weights, resistance bands, and handled bands of differing tension or resistance. A gym, while helpful, is not needed. Using body weight exercises—such as push-ups and sit-ups—can be one place to start. There are a few examples of body weight exercise routines in the Appendices.

A personal trainer or gym might be a place to get ideas on how to get started. Generally, an evaluation of where you are physiologically is a good idea, and your personal physician should be consulted. In fact, your physician might be able to recommend who you should talk to for a beginning routine as well. The important thing is to start something low intensity and then progressively but gradually increase the routine over time. The important thing is to start. As we say in running, the toughest step is the first one—out the door—but the key is to start. You might like it, and perhaps it might create some opportunities for socialization (such as a running group). As you progress, you might find that a gym or personal trainer can be of assistance. However, this is an individual determination that is not needed to initiate a fitness program. The key message is to START.

Cardio is also part of any exercise routine. Walking, even in place, is a place to begin. Then increase your pace and/or length of walk once your stamina improves. If you can tolerate it, run. Biking is also an option. A stationary bike can help, but if the logistics are favorable, biking outside will work. The key is to find a routine and a set of exercises that fit your schedule and physical level. Then once you're doing it, you can modify the progression and the exercises. An ancillary benefit of an exercise program is that it increases your metabolic rate throughout the day and you tend to burn more calories.

Everyone should be more physically fit, but what's important is to get started.

Mental acuity. As we age, we lose some mental acuity. We need to keep our minds active to avoid or limit some of this effect. This is particularly true in what I am doing. I have found that racing keeps my mind extremely sharp, though this is not a suggestion for others. There are racing exercises that help boost our mental acuity. These exercises can also be carried out as part of everyday life.

Other exercises can assist here. I was with my girlfriend's children on Christmas Day 2020 and they reluctantly sucked me into playing a video game, which I viewed as a worthless time-consuming endeavor. However, I found that once I changed my attitude and got into the game, my performance improved. I also found myself trying to outsmart the game's algorithm. This was a form of mental exercise that I could translate to my racing and improve my mental reflexes in the process. Anyone can use these games to improve their mental acuity.

Juggling can also assist in mental acuity; many top-notch race drivers do it. Juggle three tennis balls and see. Start with fewer balls at first or even just one ball at a time. Once coordination improves, add another ball and work up to three balls.

Diet. Many different things directly impact your health—including your genetic code, your access to health care, and your place of residence. But the best thing you can do to stay healthy is to follow healthy eating habits. That means consuming large numbers of fruits, vegetables, whole grains, and legumes (beans). The U.S. Department of Agriculture recommends two cups of fruit every day (Americans, on average, consume a little more than one cup daily). And the goal should be to eat these foods in their natural (or minimally processed) form. Whole oranges, for example, are much better for you than orange juice—since juice lacks the fiber that's an essential part of a healthy diet.

This can also be conveyed as a negative. In the United States, diet is the leading risk factor for death. That's because poor food choices contribute to most of the leading causes of death, such as heart disease and cancer.

You probably have a good idea of what's healthy and what's not. But with unhealthy food temptations all around us, how to resist them? There are no easy answers, but here are a few tips:

First, eat restaurant food as little as possible. More than 96 percent of the entrées offered at chain restaurants exceed USDA recommended per-meal limits for sodium, fat, and saturated fat, according to a study published in 2013. The portion sizes are also much larger than just about anyone should be eating. (A recent study showed that since 1986, calorie counts of fast-food entrée items and desserts had grown 27 percent and 79 percent, respectively.) The restaurants make them large because it doesn't cost much for them to do so, and it leads consumers to think they're getting a good deal. The reality is they're just getting a larger waistline.

Second, cook at home. The best way to take control of what you're eating is to cook it yourself, with natural ingredients along the lines of those I listed above. (And putting a frozen meal in the microwave or oven doesn't count as "cooking.") Yes, it takes more time. But it's better for you—and probably cheaper too.

Third, when you go to the grocery store (or shop online), don't buy unhealthy food. It's tempting to think that you'll only eat junk food in moderation, or that you'll only make it available to others. But we all know that's not true. As a diet adviser has said, "In your house, in your mouth."

Fourth, focus on fiber, not protein. It's one of the dietary myths that people need to consume large amounts of protein to be healthy. Humans need less than is commonly believed—the recommended daily allowance is 0.8 grams per 2.2 pounds of body weight—and it's almost impossible to be protein deficient. (Also remember that plant-based foods also have plenty of protein.) What we do need a lot of is fiber—and an estimated 95 percent of Americans are deficient in this area. Foods high in fiber include beans, peas, quinoa, and raspberries. Foods with no fiber include red meat, chicken, fish, eggs, and cheese.

Fifth, try to limit your beverages to tea and water, and maybe an occasional beer or glass of wine. Soda—whether diet or not—is unhealthy. Also unhealthy are energy drinks like Red Bull and sports drinks like Gatorade. Drink lots of water. When I wake up, I try to drink a liter of water and then drink water throughout the day. The body gets dehydrated overnight so water first thing can help. Water throughout the day helps you be hydrated and an ancillary benefit is you feel fuller and maybe less likely to eat, snack, or nibble.

Sixth, don't eat while watching TV. It's too easy to lose track of what you're eating, which leads to overconsumption. A study by two Ohio State University professors compared the incidence of obesity among more than 12,000 adults who always watched TV during family meals compared to those who never did. The TV viewers had 37 percent higher odds of obesity.

Seventh, be discerning in the studies you read about food. There's a lot of junk science out there, backed by the food industry. While not everything is known, of course, we do have a good idea of what's good for you and what's not. For example, a study by Harvard professors that tracked the dietary habits of more than 120,000 American men and women for twenty years showed that the foods most strongly associated with weight loss were yogurt, nuts, and fruits. The foods most strongly associated with weight gain were French fries, potato chips, and sugar-sweetened beverages.

Eighth, know your dietary nemesis. Mine is ice cream. However, I have mentally figured out how to discipline myself. I used to binge eat ice cream but now I only have ice cream once every 2–3 months and when I do I consciously control the portions. You should find your nemesis and figure out how to control it.

What happens if you don't follow any of this advice? That depends on several different factors, including genetics, whether you exercise, and precisely what you're eating. But an unhealthy diet certainly increases the likelihood of becoming obese. And since so much of this book involves cars, I'm including one writer's observation—Greg Critser, author of *Fat Land: How Americans Became the Fattest People in the World*— that the body of a human is like the body of a car:

> The obese body is like a four-cylinder car pulling a trailer full of bricks: it is, in the simplest sense, overloaded. Its cylinders—the heart and its ancillary arteries and veins—are not built for pulling the extra weight, and must work harder, straining to accommodate the load. Its fuel injection system—the pancreas, the liver, and all of the organs that process fuel—are similarly overloaded, unable to process enough energy or to get it to the proper places to fire the body's key muscles. Its chassis—the skeleton—groansnder the excess weight, and like a car with bad shocks it begins to jangle and bump with the most minute movements.

That's not a car I would want to drive every day—and certainly not a body I would want to live with. You hopefully feel the same way. Eating healthy is the best way to prevent this scenario from being realized. As someone smarter than me once said, "Nothing tastes as good as healthy feels."

We each need to evolve a positive attitude. Sometimes that's difficult to do when we are working, dealing with other problems, or facing family issues. However, having a positive view can improve our situation and our attitude. We each are in control of what we do for ourselves and with our bodies. I have chosen an activity I enjoy, which makes it easy to stay motivated. We can each make these choices. Exercise doesn't have to cost anything, so we don't need much money to do it.

So, why not do something? Your physical condition will improve, your mental acuity might improve, and—if you eat right — your weight will improve. All of these improvements are likely to lead your outlook to improve as well. All pluses. Give it a try

39

The Chapter

"There is only one corner of the universe you can be certain of improving, and that's your own self."

Aldous Huxley

"For a man to conquer himself is the first and noblest of all victories."

Plato

"Decision-making, like coffee, needs a cooling process."

George Washington

One of the keys to successful racing is remembering that you can't control what other drivers are doing—you can only control yourself. Indeed, this is the essence of driving fast—being in control of yourself. That means not getting flustered when something goes wrong. Put differently, you must become comfortable with being uncomfortable. Racing at high speeds is often an uncomfortable experience when you first start doing it. But the more you do it, and the more you understand the ins and outs of what you're doing, the more comfortable you'll be.

The importance of being in control of yourself was brought home to me when I was writing the previous chapter about racing and aging. While working on that chapter one Saturday, I was experiencing a surge in creativity. At the end of the day, I figured I'd take a break and return to the chapter the following day. When I did, I was full of enthusiasm and after a few hours I finished it off. I was so proud of myself. I reread the chapter and I really liked it.

I picked up the mail late Saturday but did not open it. When I did, I found a note from a friend, with an article based on an interview with NASCAR racer Jimmy Johnson. The article focused on his switch from driving NASCARs to IndyCars and his new exercise program (which he said he disliked), while also mentioning his age (forty-five) and his diet. This struck me because the chapter I had just finished covered some of this territory including exercise, mental acuity, and diet—all in the context of aging.

Having just finished my chapter covering similar topics, and given that my friend and I had been communicating about racing and diet and exercise, I decided to email him a copy of the new chapter. I opened the manuscript and copied the chapter and then went into my emails to send to him. However, when I clicked the paste application nothing appeared. I figured that I just messed up in the copy process, which was correct. But when

I went back into the manuscript to recopy the chapter, I found that the chapter was GONE!

I panicked. I looked and looked for it but in the end it was deleted. I called my friend in an effort to see if somewhere in the Word software another copy existed—to no avail. Very frustrating.

I had many thoughts about what to do. I had a busy Sunday afternoon planned and was wondering about those plans. I considered that maybe the book didn't need that chapter anyway (I would essentially give up) and that I should leave it out. I subsequently concluded that it was relevant to the book and that there should be something covering those topics.

The experience I was encountering reminded me of a time when I was racing at Watkins Glen with a guy named Peter. We were on the same team but driving separate cars. Peter was a waiter in a restaurant in South Florida and had run into a customer in the restaurant named Bob (not his real name) who was a professional NASCAR driver. Out of that conversation, Peter found out Bob was racing at Watkins Glen the same weekend as us and then solicited Bob to drive as his co-driver, for no cost. Bob agreed since he was going to be there the same weekend and had all his expenses paid and wanted the extra track time—a win-win.

Peter went out in the first practice (since Bob had already driven the track in his NASCAR ride) and when he went into a section called the bus stop, he hit dirt on the track from another competitor, lost control, and went directly into the tire barrier. Peter was unhurt but the car was badly damaged in the front. The team brought the car back to the paddock and attempted to repair it. They concluded the damage was too extensive to be repaired in the limited time available. Peter's plan had just evaporated.

I was chatting with Bob and was saying how I felt bad for Peter given that he didn't have a lot or money and had brokered the deal that Bob would drive with him, and it was Peter's chance for success to have Bob as his co-driver. Bob responded unsympathetically: "He has no one to blame but himself." How true.

I found myself in exactly the same position with the deleted chapter. I was sort of staring at myself in the mirror. I, and I alone, was to blame for my situation. That's when I realized I needed to get back into control and think more rationally. I decided to fix the situation and rewrite the chapter, since the points in that chapter needed to be made. The material was as fresh in my mind as it was ever going to be. So I spent the next three hours doing the rewrite. When I finished it again, I was happy with it.

If this had occurred years earlier, I would have spent a ton of time cursing and complaining and maybe even given up. But now I've come to have a more grounded and realistic perspective. I make sure not to catastrophize the situation.

I calmly began the rewrite, trying as much as possible to reconstruct the points that I recalled were in the original chapter. Clearly, I had messed up. I was angry with myself and my desire to attend to my afternoon plans didn't help.

The flaw in my approach was that I was only using a single manuscript copy, making the changes to that version, and adding chapters directly into that manuscript. The only thing I was changing was the date. That clearly exposed me to the risk of something happening. I immediately started writing additional chapters in separate files and updating the manuscript as I placed each new chapter into the manuscript. I also sent a copy of the manuscript to my friend for safekeeping.

The lessons here are varied. When things like this occur, calm down. Don't get frustrated. When they do occur, do something to calm yourself. (Calling my friend helped calm me down.)

I wouldn't have been able to do what I did in this situation when I was younger. A more impulsive/reactive me would not have been calm and might have simply given up. Perhaps I have learned. Or perhaps I'm more laser focused on the objective—the book or message or points to be made. In racing, we try to stay calm; we even use calming techniques that are highly individualized. Whatever it takes, we each need to think, stay calm, and allow our thoughts about what to do emerge.

Most of the time we know the answer or action to take; it's just that the stress or emotions suppress those thoughts. Controlling your feelings can lead to those thoughts emerging. Things will improve.

40

Think Before You Act

"Valor withers without adversity."

Seneca

"In the middle of difficulty lies opportunity."

Albert Einstein

I was racing at Watkins Glen. I'm quite familiar with the track and I was anticipating a good performance. At the time, I was in a battle for the regional championship and it was one of a few "out of region" races in the series. My main competitor was in the race and he and I were always battling over who was going to win. At the time, I was in the lead for the regional championship.

I was always trying to get better, and my crew was telling me to push the limit. Before the big Sunday race that weekend, my crew chief asked when I had last slid off the track.

"I can't remember," I replied.

He said that sliding off the track is not necessarily a good thing, but it helps define when you are going as fast as or faster than you should through the corner. It is corner speed that makes you fast for the lap.

I drove extremely well during the race and had a large lead as I passed the start-finish line on my last lap. For some inexplicable reason, the thought of pushing the limit came into my head. I went into the first turn and carried more speed than normal. The left front tire went over the outside exit curb and onto the grass leaving my right front tire on the asphalt, and because the front wheels were slightly turned to the right, the car went across track to the right and struck the tire wall. The car came to a halt and I was having trouble getting it started. The other cars passed me. I finally managed to get the car started again, and I passed all but two of the other cars, so I finished third.

We were in the impound area and my crew chief came up to me and said, "You know how I have been telling you to find the limit?"

"Yes," I responded.

"That's it," he said.

This episode was an example of me pushing the limit. But losing the race cost me the championship. That hurt, but it was self-inflicted. I should have thought about what I was doing before I did it. Perhaps it was the heat of battle. Or maybe I was just not thinking at all. The better play would have been to be cautious, win the race, and push the limit at a safer time and place. I should have thought through what I was doing before doing it.

The moral of the story is to think before you act and have patience when making your choices. I did not consult with the crew—they cannot help while you are on the track. I just did it. I should have been patient and pushed the limit another time.

In our personal and professional lives, we need to be patient and think through our choices. Make sure you know what's on the line in making a particular decision. The result of that decision could impact something larger than you think in the moment.

41

Why Do We Do This?

"Keep your eyes on the stars, and your feet on the ground."
Theodore Roosevelt

"One of the things I learned the hard way was that it doesn't pay to get discouraged. Keeping busy and making optimism a way of life can restore your faith in yourself."
Lucille Ball

"Our greatest weakness lies in giving up. The most certain way to succeed is always to try just one more time."
Thomas Edison

In late September 2021, our team decided that we would enter the 24 Hours of Daytona race in January 2022. Having competed in the race in January 2021, we knew what was involved. We reached the seventeen-hour mark, at which point we had a transmission shifting issue that prevented us from continuing. Had this issue not arisen, we would have completed the race.

The other drivers on our team helped minimize my workload—a smart move since they were all in better physical condition than me and also had more racing experience. Four months before the 2021 race, I had begun an augmented workout program.

To prepare for the 2022 race, we decided to participate in the HRS (Historic Racing Series) Classic 24 Hour race at the Daytona International Speedway in October 2021. It is a series of practices and sprint races that culminates with the Classic 24—a series of one-hour races within a twenty-four hour period. It represents a test of driving at varying times of day. In doing so we experienced driving at dusk, night, and dawn, dealing with the sunrise, sunset, and high speeds, driving when tired with limited amounts of sleep, etc. It's as much of a physical and mental test as it is of driving skill.

For this event we had another team run the car. This team had done the same for us at the 2021 24 Hours of Daytona race. In that race, we augmented their crew, with our crew doing the over the wall work—tire changes and refueling—since our guys are fast. Also, since we had worked with that team before, we had experience with their crew members (our crew members were the same). Because they had much more experience in the 24 Hours of Daytona, our learning curve shrank, giving us the best chance for a good result.

We developed a plan to approach the 2021 Classic 24. This included having one of my co-drivers, Hugh, give me a break if needed. He drove the first sprint practice as normal, mostly to baseline the speed of the car and to ensure things were working properly. In this event we had decided to use the actual Rolex 24 car to help me get accustomed to the car, the track, and the environment. The previous year we had used another slower car, but this year it was more like a real dress rehearsal.

As the week progressed, I drove in the sprint practices and the sprint races. I was on a normal trajectory of increased speed and lowering lap times, and I was running better than my previous lap times in the same car. My goal is always to be as close to Hugh's times as possible. Being close to the other drivers translates to flexibility in the driver rotation in the real races, and enables the strategists to optimize driver rotation—matching us with the rotation of other teams so that we drive when other drivers of similar times are in the other cars.

Drivers also need to drive at different times of day with limited rest, but still be able to maintain their driving performance. In order to do so, we must be in good physical shape and be able to acclimate to driving at times that are contrary to our individual circadian rhythms.

The Classic 24 was going to be a test of how I adapted to the environmental changes. My plan was to drive as many of the sessions and races as I felt I could handle, with the goal being to drive them all. As the week progressed, we were continually evaluating my performance and testing my conditioning.

The Classic 24 is held after all the sprint races. Its one-hour races are divided by classes that begin Saturday afternoon and then cycle through the next twenty-four hours on a rotating basis. My one-hour races were at 5 p.m., 10 p.m., 5 a.m., and 10 a.m. Racing at 175 mph when you're tired and it's dark doesn't sound too bad, right?

Whether I would race at 5 a.m. depended on how I felt after the 10 p.m. race. In the event I felt tired, Hugh's preference was to skip the 5 a.m. race if I didn't feel right rather than have him drive to try to keep us up on the leader board.

At 11 p.m. Saturday I felt pretty good. Of course, we needed to discount that at that moment I was infused with adrenaline, which would wear off with the passage of time. We decided that I would get a little sleep and see how I felt at around 2:30 a.m. We had to be at the track at least an hour before each race. The crew would be sticking around longer after my race and arriving before me, so they were getting even less rest.

When I woke up at 3 a.m. I felt pretty alert and good, so I drove the full race at 5 a.m. Throughout the previous races I had been improving my lap times, to the point where I was within about 3 seconds of Hugh (and this race continued that trend). In January 2021, my fastest time was a 1:54, compared to Hugh's 1:47. Now I was in the 1:50s compared to Hugh's 1:47. Not bad.

We decided I would also give the 10 a.m. race a try. I ended up running the fastest times of the week on used tires—nearly a 1:50 flat, which was the closest I have been to Hugh at this track in this car. This came after all the other races, but I didn't feel that bad physically. My favorite compliment came from Mike, my car chief, who said, "You're a different driver than you were in January." That meant a lot to me because I am continually working on improving my conditioning and driving abilities.

Sometimes when we are progressing (assuming we are progressing) in minor increments we don't notice the changes. That's why it's so valuable to get an assessment from someone who hasn't been seeing your performance, particularly someone who is in the racing business.

So why did I do it? To prove to myself that I could. As a test of whether my conditioning was working. To demonstrate to myself that I could drive as much as I could without any degradation in performance. Testing myself for the real event. It was the closest experience I could get to replicating the 24 Hours of Daytona, and I passed.

Before and during the event I had some doubts about whether I could do it, but I had the confidence and certainly the support of folks around me. If I am satisfied with my performance, that's what really matters. But it's helpful if others recognize what you are doing, as it gives you encouragement for the future. This speaks to the importance of surrounding yourself with people who can provide objective input and encouragement when the need is there.

There were two other drivers (on another team) running an identical car to ours. Both drivers were ten to fifteen years younger than me. They shared the driving stints in their car and neither drove the 5 a.m. race. I had driven all the races and stints alone. Even so, I was never comparing myself to them—only myself to myself and what I thought I could achieve.

.

42

Life Is Full of Disappointments but in the End You Look Forward

"Sometimes you're the windshield, sometimes you're the bug."

Mary Chapin Carpenter

We were at Road Atlanta for the final race of the 2021 IMSA season, with high hopes that our cars were prepped and ready to take on the competition. We were racing the Camaros—the 46 for Hugh and Matt and the 64 for Owen and myself. We were still dealing with a disadvantage: IMSA had forced us to reduce the power in our cars. (As discussed earlier, the race series attempts to equalize the cars on-track, and they can reduce power, add weight, adjust ride height, or make other

211

adjustments in this process.) We persevered, but drove the cars hard. The result was various parts failures: half shafts, transmissions, differentials, etc.

The 46 car had qualified fifth on the third row, which was a good place to start. Our car qualified seventeenth, but still in a good position.

After the start, the 46 car was running lap times comparable to the cars ahead of it. In fact, the crew did a great job with the pit stop and the car came out of the pit in second place. We knew it might need to make another stop for a splash of fuel unless accidents led to some double yellow pace car laps.

The 64 car had a great stop as well. After the stops, Owen was driving well and catching up to the 46 car, which was now in third place. Owen was faster than the 46 car and we envisioned that he would soon catch it and possibly pass it. The 64 car was running faster lap times than the race leader so it appeared that we could win the race. If so, this would be my first class win in the pro series, which had always been a goal of mine. Suddenly, it looked like we could have two cars in the top five at least, with perhaps both cars on the podium and one winning the race. That would be a great way to finish off the season.

The team was feeling great, and this would have been my first podium with a Chevy plus my first win. It could have been at least a P2 finish had we passed the 46 car. The 46 car was racing well and almost surely in position to finish on the podium, so things seemed set there.

As the 64 was catching up going into Turn 10A (a tight left-hand turn at the end of a long straightaway), it was tapped by another car from the right side (the cars were side by side). Turn 10A is followed very quickly by a tight right-hand turn—Turn

10B. As our car was exiting Turn 10B, it drifted to the left and went off-track slightly and the left side tires went into a gravel trap. As our car reentered the track, it ran over a curb, which dislodged the rear bumper on the right rear. We tried to shake the bumper, to no avail. Eventually, the race officials made us stop to tear the bumper off. We were suddenly out of contention, falling from fifth to tenth—or, as we say, from "hero to zero" in a split second.

But we knew the 46 car was still in a great position to finish on the podium. And a few laps later they were able to hold off a few cars from behind, which enabled them to finish third. We were on the podium and there was a tremendous celebration for the team. We sprayed champagne and our fans cheered. We couldn't have asked for a better finish to our race season.

After a race, the cars of the top five finishers go through a technical inspection—normally this inspection can include weighing the cars or anything else in the rules. After about an hour, we learned that we had failed the tech inspection—our car was eight pounds below the minimum weight. Suddenly, we were not third but were disqualified. Disqualification meant I needed to return the trophies because they were not rightfully ours. A very difficult thing to do.

This roller coaster cycle is a lot like what we experience in life, with lots of highs and lows. To try to figure out what happened, we slowed down and started to analyze what went wrong. We looked at event television coverage and our own videos to analyze what occurred. Did the side contact damage the 64 car? What occurred to make the car go off-track? Then we worked through steps for the 46 car. Was it weighed before the race? Who weighed it? What scales were used? Were the scales calibrated properly and when? Understanding where things got messed up was the only rational way to envision a path forward. Even in disappointment, we must think logically and rationally.

As I have continually mentioned, with any event or situation that occurs, positive or negative, you must always look to what was causal to the positive or negative result or effect. In positive situations, you do it so you understand why it occurred and what can be done to sustain it or improve the result. In the negative, you want to learn from your mistakes. You always learn more from your mistakes than you do from your successes—if you allow it. However, in any negative situation, what you cannot do is give up or stop. You evaluate, learn, understand, reposition, plan, and then look forward and move on.

43

The Crew—NOTHING Happens without Them

"If everyone is moving forward together, then success takes care of itself."

Henry Ford

Throughout this book, you have heard again and again about the cars and the drivers. But you should have also picked up on members of the crew and the critical role they play in the success of a race team, or any team. Anything that needs to be done needs to be in someone's job description. And each team member is relied upon to do their assigned tasks, do them timely, and do them well. Any issues will diminish the whole team's performance.

In racing, the most discussed team members are the drivers. Yes, each driver is a team member. The driver's role, beyond just driving, is to help prepare the car to be properly set up, since every race environment and every track differ. The starting driver is the qualifying driver. The main job of the starting driver in the race is to keep a good pace (in other words, don't fall a lap behind the overall race leaders) and prevent the car from being damaged so that the next driver will be able to close the race with decent equipment.

The strength of the team members lies in their commitment and dedication to their respective jobs. This is key because there are safety issues at play here. If there are mechanical issues with the car during a race, the outcome can endanger the life of the driver—and other drivers in the race. So these issues need to be avoided at all costs.

CREW CHIEF

There is usually a hierarchy among the crew members, with the crew chief at the top. This is the individual to whom the team reports and whose responsibility it is to understand everything related to the car's performance.

MECHANICS

Key to the team are the mechanics. There is usually a lead mechanic of each car (sometimes called a "car chief") and he is responsible for ensuring the car is in compliance with the team's safety standards and the race series rules.

RACE ENGINEERS

The race engineers are usually mechanical engineers who understand the machinal workings of the car. They work with the drivers during car setup. They evaluate what the car is doing via feedback, and use that information to pinpoint the appropriate setup for the car, based on the track, the weather, and other conditions.

Once the setup adjustments are identified, the mechanics are told what changes to make. These can include spring rate changes, ride height changes, changes in camber and caster, changes in the sway bar settings, etc. Usually, the mechanics report back that the changes have been made and the engineer typically maintains a log of what has been done and what the results have been. To do this, there is usually a meeting after each on-track session, during which the success or failure of the changes is evaluated and discussed.

RACE STRATEGISTS

There are race strategists on the team whose role is to monitor the race's progress, understanding where the team's cars are in the mix, understanding the relative position of the competitors' cars, monitoring pits stops by other cars and their duration (and whether they have taken fuel and swapped out tires and drivers), tracking the fuel burn of our cars and an estimate for the other cars, etc. This complex mix of data points needs to be synthesized to inform the race strategy decisions about when to stop and why. Endurance racing is a thinking game even more so than a driving exercise.

TIRE ENGINEERS

Tires are critically important. The tire engineers and crew chief determine which tires to use for which session and when they should be changed.

New tires have more grip. Maximal grip typically occurs around lap 3–5, but then can table off quickly. Several different factors need to be considered. For example, the car could be set up to achieve a maximal race lap speed, but doing so will diminish the tire's grip. Given that this is endurance racing, being consistently better over a longer time is better than being fast for a shorter period. Therefore, the race engineers typically test for a long tire run to measure the tire degradation. Occasionally they will decide that faster over a shorter period might be better, so they will test for that too. The more information you have about all the different variables, the better will be your decisions.

RACE FUEL

Someone is typically tasked with obtaining the required race fuel. Fuel rigs that hold up to fifty-five gallons are in the pits. They need to pass a technical inspection for safety and for height. Yes, the height is regulated; the higher the rig, the faster the fuel flow. It's the job of the fuel crew members to stay on top of this. In many situations, this individual also drives the race hauler (a tractor trailer) and/or a separate parts truck and trailer. And it is not uncommon for the fuel team to also be tire crew members as well.

OVER THE WALL CREW

These crew members perform the pit stops, and they typically have other responsibilities. The roles are one jack man, one fueler, and two tire changers. There is typically a limit on the number of crew who can be over the wall during a pit stop. Therefore, in a crisis, such as the car needing emergency service, the number of crew needs to be managed. Each crew member has a radio, and the strategist or crew chief will call the instructions for the stop. These crew members are selected for their respective tasks, and they are trained and then practice doing the stops. As mentioned in a prior chapter, "only perfect practice makes perfect." Therefore, these folks practice doing the right things fast once they have been trained.

For perspective, it takes about 52–55 seconds to fuel the car from near empty, 24–26 seconds to complete the driver change, and 24–26 seconds to change all four tires. The fuel is the limiting factor, since it takes the longest. So generally, it's better to slow down the tires and driver change to get them error free. However, in the event the fuel tank is not empty (typically because of an on-track incident occurred and they needed to slow the racing down to get things cleaned up), and the tires or drivers are being changed, the time period is shortened for changing the driver and the tires.

Many crew members have worked on our race team. One of them, Dave Modderman, is a good illustration of what crew members do and the dedication they have. He had previously been part of another team and had even gone with them to Le Mans for the 24 Hours race.

Dave was our rear-tire changer as well as a mechanic. During one race several years ago, we were driving a BMW, and to make it fast we ran it with very soft springs and very soft shock settings. When the car came in for a pit stop, the jack man jacked up the left side of the car and of course both wheels were off the ground. But because of the soft springs and soft shock settings, the wheels sagged. Consequently, there was a lot of space between the top of the tire and the body of the car.

Once Dave was finished changing the left rear tire, he put his right hand on the top of the tire to support himself while he stood up. Unfortunately, the jack man thought Dave was clear and dropped the jack, which caught Dave's forearm between the body and the tire with no space in between.

Dave squealed in pain, which caused the jack man to recognize what had happened. He immediately raised the jack and Dave pulled his arm out. Noticeably injured, Dave nonetheless went around to the right side of the car and changed that tire, using only one hand and using the injured arm to support the right-side tire he was putting on.

Once finished, Dave was taken immediately to medical and then to the hospital—his arm was broken and needed pins so it could be put back together. This dedication is not uncommon among crew members and racers. Dave realized that the pit stop depended on him completing his work then and there so the car could leave.

This situation has parallels to everyday life. Sometimes we need to persevere and get things done in very adverse and trying circumstances—and we surprise ourselves (and others) by what we can accomplish in these circumstances.

The need for teamwork and coordination in racing is no different than in other sports or even in the workplace. Every team member needs to be relied upon to do their respective job, do it timely, and do it well. But teams in racing are a bit like teams in medicine—the stakes are extremely high, given that mistakes can have lethal consequences. Thus, it is essential for each role to be properly executed.

44

Strong Showings—
Very Strong

"Never discourage anyone who continually makes progress, no matter how slow."

Plato

"Success seems to be connected with action. Successful people keep moving. They make mistakes, but they don't quit."

Conrad Hilton

"Train yourself to let go of everything you fear to lose."

Yoda

Four drivers for TGM were competing in the January 2022 Michelin Pilot Challenge Series: Owen and myself in the 64 car and Hugh and Matt in the 46 car. We were racing at Daytona International Speedway in our new Porsche GT4 RS Clubsports. The practices went well and Owen and I finished second. Owen drove much of the four-hour race and did so without air conditioning, which gave him a little more power on the course's high-speed banking. At the finish, he was so dehydrated and exhausted that he needed medical attention, which prevented him from joining me on the podium.

It's a longstanding tradition in racing for those on the podium to spray champagne, which is why they typically have the bottles uncorked and opened. I happily sprayed the champagne. (It had been quite some time since I was on an IMSA podium.) Soon thereafter I realized that I had Owen's bottle, which was still intact. So I grabbed it and sprayed the others, and they could not spray anything back. The next day, Owen and I made up for his absence by having our pictures taken together on the podium. A great feeling indeed.

The next day—Saturday, January 29, 2022—marked the start of the 24 Hours of Daytona race. We were the only four drivers from the same team to run the Michelin race on Friday and then turn around and compete in the twenty-four-hour race. (These races are a test of endurance for the drivers as much as for the cars.)

Having raced in the 24 Hours of Daytona in 2021 and only completing seventeen hours before a mechanical issue prevented us from finishing, our goal was simply to complete the twenty-four hours. For the second year in a row, we partnered with a well-known Porsche race team that had considerable experience in the Rolex race. I had prepared by participating in several other races that approximated the endurance of the Rolex race. But they were nothing like the real twenty-four-hour race.

Our race strategy focused on who would drive when, though driver rotation is always subject to change depending on the circumstances. Since I was the slower of the four drivers, as in the prior race, the team decided I would start—and do so in the rear of the field since it is the safest place from which to start.

The race began at 1:30 p.m. and I had a reasonably fast but otherwise uneventful stint that lasted about 55–60 minutes (that's when the car's fuel is exhausted).

In a twenty-four-hour race, the toughest times are during the night. If you make it through the night, you have a good chance of finishing. And once you have the finish in sight, you can actually begin racing. So the initial objective is survival.

Earlier, I quoted the popular racing observation that "in order to finish first you must first finish." The race is never won in the first turn but is often lost there. After my stint went off without incident, Hugh drove, and then I got behind the wheel again. When I was finished, I planned to go to the motorhome and get some rest.

Before doing so, I saw on the monitor that Matt was hit by a Lamborghini in our class. Our left rear wheel was badly damaged, as was the body work on the left quarter panel. The car limped around the track, costing us time, but eventually made it to the pits. The crew broke out the Bear Bond (which is kind of like duct tape on steroids) and patched up the car. The car was functional if not too pretty. The Bear Bond was reapplied during the next pit stop since it was flapping in the wind.

The collision with the Lamborghini resulted in our right-side mirror being knocked off. That meant we lost the ability to see cars passing on our right. However, we still had our spotters and the rearview camera as well as the convex mirror in the center of the windshield. Limping back to the pits, coupled with the repair stops, cost us a few laps.

It was evening when I finally made it to the motorhome. Owen was driving and I saw on the television coverage that he was in the infield and up against the tire wall. Making matters worse, the car would not go into reverse, so he had to wait to be towed backwards before he could go. He also had a flat left front tire (likely the cause of the off-track incident) and had to limp most of the way around the track to get to the pits, costing us at least two laps or more. The crew replaced the left front tire and checked the car over. Before long, off he went again.

Early the next morning I got back into the car for a few stints. The first was the sunrise stint. While the setting can be beautiful, at 180 mph there's no time for looking around and taking in the scenery. And when you are headed east around the banking, the sun is intense for a few seconds—blinding the driver's view. It's also bad coming out of Turn 1 and Turn 3—both of which look east. While we have sun visors on our helmets, the sun remains a challenge.

Shortly after my stint started, I noticed that the left-side mirror was also gone (no one had told me). I knew there was nothing that could be done about it, so I just had to deal with it and drive on. You drive the best you can with what you have.

"Just keep doing what you're doing," the crew was telling me.

I was about two seconds per lap faster than I had been the year before. After a break of about two hours, I started driving again. This time I was running even faster lap times, getting closer in lap times to my pro teammates. Again, "keep doing what you're doing" was the call from the pit. The spotter is with you the entire time and coaches you through traffic. Each driver needs to be behind the wheel at least four and a half hours. Toward the end of my second stint, the crew chief asked if I could drive another 20–30 minutes (this would get me over my minimum drive time requirement). When I said yes, they had me stop for more fuel and sent me back out on the same tires. During this latter stint I was running my fastest lap times for the race. This was important to me and the team since it meant that I had the physical endurance to keep driving without a degradation in performance.

When the race started, we were in sixty-first place overall and twenty-second in our class. We steadily moved up. With about six laps remaining, we were in seventh in our class. Looking good.

As we neared the end of the race, Matt said that I should be driving at the finish. I told him that if my driving would mean losing a position then we shouldn't do it. He responded that while he was one of the most competitive guys on the planet, he still thought that I should finish the race even if it meant losing a position. (Everyone on our team is fiercely competitive.) But I held on to seventh place, which wasn't difficult since the eighth-place car was six laps behind us. Driving through the checkered flag felt great after such a long race and such a great performance by everyone on the team—drivers and crew alike.

When I finished the race, the team and the crew were elated. My girlfriend and my two daughters as well as a few friends who attended the race were there in pit lane when I pulled in. A great feeling and a great result for TGM and me personally. We finished, and finished well, with others taking notice of our collective performance and result.

It wasn't too long before I started talking about the 24 Hours of Daytona race in 2023 and getting prepared for that one. It's the way we are.

LIFE LESSON

What does this race have to do with life and this book? A lot. I included this chapter because it represents a capstone for the message of this book. It says you develop a plan and strategy for achieving your goals. Then you begin the process and move toward your goal. It shows we don't know what things we are going to encounter, but we deal with what occurs in the best way we can with the resources we have. We prepare, persevere, progress, achieve, reposition, achieve again, and eventually attain greater performance than we imagined possible.

The message here is that quitting is not an option. Create your plan and then begin executing that plan. There will be disappointments, surprises, and unanticipated changes in the environment. But you change plans and move on—forward. You do not stop, you adjust, reposition, you continue to progress. Even if you don't achieve everything you want, you learn and that learning helps you improve and overcome the next challenge.

Several months before I added this chapter, we shared the manuscript with our publisher. The response was that we should add something about my biggest racing accomplishments. My thought was that the publisher didn't get the point of the book— my greatest racing accomplishment hadn't occurred yet. As the Frank Sinatra song says, "The best is yet to come."

Focus Forward.
Now GO FOR IT.

45

I Love This Job

"The secret of joy in work is contained in one word, excellence. To know how to do something well is to enjoy it."

Pearl S. Buck

Many of us need to work in order to make ends meet. This is the rule rather than the exception. The exception is that we feel fulfilled by what we do, we are good at it, we feel it contributes to a larger good, we like it, and we can make money at it.

When I was in consulting, I generally liked what I did, but about 95 percent of the time my work was boring and/or repetitive. But the money I earned allowed me to do the things that I loved with the other 5 percent of my time. I focused on figuring out what to do during that 5 percent—for me and for my family. And when the firm where I was working was taken over by a larger firm, I decided to go out on my own because I wanted to do things my way.

This is the everyday reality for most of us who work. In the end, we need to find something about what we do that we enjoy. It might be the people, the work, the location, the travel, or something else. However, most of us "work to live"—we don't "live to work." This means not becoming overly wedded to our jobs and not focusing too much on work. I was guilty of working too much many years ago, and it brought personal costs. Perspective and a panoramic view of your life is very much needed.

Some folks can experience depression as a result of their work situation, and they contemplate harming themselves. It is important to pivot from such thoughts and focus on the positives. There are always positives.

We all have a professional side and a personal side to our lives. I believe that you can tolerate a disruption in one of these two dimensions, but not both simultaneously. I was once in a situation where my wife had left me and I lost my job. I had nothing and I was watching my savings dwindle to almost nothing. Then one of my friends got me into cars, which gave me something to focus on. It pulled me along for a while and before long I had another job offer. In the new job I was being paid substantially less than in the previous position, but I was just happy to have a job. Soon thereafter I met a great lady who eventually became my wife. Everything worked out. I just needed to be patient for a little while.

But it's great to enjoy what you do and be good at it. Making some money at it is a nice bonus. In the end, I would like my epitaph to be a version of what Richard Petty allegedly wanted as his epitaph—"he was a man who had a job, who liked his job, and did it well." Notice this never mentions anything about money. It's really about fulfillment. I have found that if you pursue excellence in yourself, money will eventually follow too.

If we ever get to the point where we really like what we do and are good at it, what more can there be? We are all good at different parts of our lives, our activities, and the work that we undertake. We all should hope that we get some enjoyment out of what we do so that it will be an anchor for us. If we get there, that's great. However, we need to enjoy and appreciate what we have and be thankful for it.

46

Lessons Learned

"A strong positive self-image is the best possible preparation for success."

Joyce Brothers

PUT YOURSELF IN POSITION TO TAKE ADVANTAGE OF OPPORTUNITIES OR SOMEONE ELSE'S BAD LUCK

In racing and in any endeavor, it's critically important to recognize that life is a process and that things change during this process. The key is to position yourself to take advantage of situations as they evolve. Always scan the horizon for things that affect or impact your plan as well as the plans of others who are on the field with you. As opportunities arise, you will be positioned to seize them.

APPROPRIATELY ASSESS YOUR POSITION, OBJECTIVES, AND PLANS

It's important to always be monitoring your plans—personal and professional—as well as the environment in which you live, so you are prepared to make changes where appropriate. Know what things in the environment will impact your goals and objectives. As you see those things change, be ready to pivot. Also, recognize that every change in the environment will not necessarily require a change in plans. There are many times when doing nothing is the wisest option.

PRIORITIZE ACTIONS AND OPPORTUNITIES

Always have a plan and then develop tasks or objectives to facilitate those plans. But be ready to make changes as needed. Once you have your plans established, prioritize tasks you need to carry out in order to realize them. You can use various techniques like PERT (Program Evaluation Review Technique) and CPM (Critical Path Method). Once you are pursuing a plan, you will find that there are several elements that are being worked on simultaneously. However, these parts are moving at different paces. CPM is used to identify the most critical path when the completion of select tasks needs to be completed before others. This is very important to successful goal attainment.

LEVERAGE OPPORTUNITIES

Once you identify an opportunity, you must evaluate whether, how, and when you can leverage it. There could be limiting factors, such as a lack of funding or a shortage of personnel or time. In certain markets, the degree of competition might confine leveraging opportunities too. This all needs to be considered and evaluated and then incorporated into the plan.

LEARN WHEN NOT TO LEVERAGE OPPORTUNITIES—CHOOSE WISELY

Not all opportunities need to be accepted or acted upon. If opportunities will not positively impact your core objective (there will be a prime objective for what you want to achieve) don't pursue them. The business strategist Tom Peters famously said, "stick to the knitting." This means identify your core business or objective and focus on that. If you start to stray, then you could dilute your focus and you may not achieve any of your goals. In short, stay focused.

BE PREPARED FOR FAILURES OR SETBACKS

Once your plan is in place and you begin to progress down the path to completion, be prepared for setbacks. These will invariably occur no matter how well you plan and how vigilantly you monitor the potential obstacles. Do not get demoralized when things pop up. Get control of yourself and think through things logically and methodically. Ask others for ideas and consider it an opportunity or a challenge rather than a setback. Remember that there are neither good things nor bad things—it's all in how you look at them. It's the truth. I promise.

LOOK AT SETBACKS AS OPPORTUNITIES, CHALLENGES, OR LEARNING EXERCISES

As I have progressed in business, driving racecars, and in life, I have always had goals and aspirations. I have also been committed to improving myself. I find that if I focus on improving me, the me versus the other guy (be they racing competitors or businesses) always takes care of itself. If I improve me and they don't, I'll get ahead. I also see setbacks as opportunities. You can reposition and learn new or different things. As I have aged, I find I need to do more to stay in shape, physically and mentally. I like to look at aging not as physiology but rather as a state of mind. I have found that *you can teach an old dog new tricks.* The main thing is that *the old dog needs to hang out with puppies.* Yes, we need to absorb the vitality of younger folks to provoke us mentally and physically. When we do this, we will think and act younger, which is really good for us.

BE CREATIVE IN YOUR APPROACH TO YOUR ENDEAVORS

Creativity is the spice of life. It means you change and grow and expand. You get this from others, reading books, the internet, and reading across a wide variety of fields and subjects. As I wrote in chapter 5, Walt Disney was once at a gathering of animated picture studios and was talking to the other studios who were asking him what he was working on. He told them. Afterwards, his staff pulled him aside and said, "Walt you told them everything we are working on."

"Yes, that's right," he responded.

One staff member asked, "Aren't you afraid they will steal those ideas?"

To which Walt responded, "*I can create faster than they can steal.*"

I mention this again because it has always stuck with me. I accepted this as a philosophical underpinning of my businesses and racing. If you keep on innovating, you will stay ahead of your competitors, whomever they are.

FOCUS FORWARD

This is a critical component to success. In racing, we tell folks that the windshield is much bigger than the mirrors. The reason? That's where you're going. In life, as in racing, where you look determines where you'll go. Research tells us that if we focus on something, we will invariably achieve that goal or objective. Focus is why. Having said that, we should not have absolute focus to the point that we have tunnel vision. We need to keep those other things in our field of view. But focus will get us to our objective.

NEVER GIVE UP

To be successful, you need determination and perseverance (sometimes known as "stick-to-it-iveness"). It takes tons of energy, which is why you need to be physically fit too. Work toward having high energy. You can do it. Remember that *the race is not always to the swift but to those who keep on running*. Once you know your plan, you need to continually evaluate it while focusing on how you're going to achieve it. You should not block out other dimensions of your life, like family or relationships, because you need them too. But the determination to attain a goal is a vital asset that can overpower things that might inhibit goal attainment. Balance is key.

CHAPTER 47

Goals and Aspirations: A Wish for You

"Ephemeralization—doing a lot with a little or doing more with less."

Buckminster Fuller

"Ask what makes you come alive and go do it. Because what the world needs is people who have come alive."

Howard Thurman

"Do not seek to follow in the footsteps of others, instead, seek what they sought."

Matsuo Basho

"Once you make a decision, the universe conspires to make it happen."

Ralph Waldo Emerson

"Live as if you were to die tomorrow. Learn as if you were to live forever."

Mahatma Gandhi

BE PRODUCTIVE IN LIFE

Be productive and be good at what you do and enjoy it. If you achieve these you will feel fulfilled. What more could you ask for? Notice I never mentioned money. I have never done things for the money. It was primarily fulfillment and doing things a certain way. In other pursuits, I found that the money followed, and more importantly, I was fulfilled.

LOVE SOMEONE AND BE LOVED BY SOMEONE

We all need someone to love. It sounds corny but humans are built for companionship and partnership. We all need someone to be with, to share with, and to love. Perhaps the greatest thing we can experience is being with the "right" person. It gives us purpose and fulfills us. If we make a mistake in this area, we may need to correct it. But that does not mean that we should not pursue another relationship.

BE GIVING

No matter what you do, have a giving, caring heart. Be compassionate. I'm not suggesting that you give folks everything you have or that you give them whatever they ask for. But when you are convinced someone needs help, do what you can—even if it's just to provide moral support.

HELP SOMEONE

Many of us get into situations where we need a little help, but many of us are afraid to ask for it. Perhaps it's our pride, our ego, or something else. If you see a situation in which someone needs help, think about if that were you or your wife or your children— would you want someone to assist them? Even if it's changing a flat tire or stopping just to call someone to assist them, that could be a big help to them. It could also allay some of their stress.

DREAM DREAMS AND SACRIFICE TO MAKE THEM COME TRUE

Do not be afraid to dream of things that should be but aren't—whether in work or in our private lives. As Robert Kennedy once said, "Some men see things as they are and say why. I dream of things that never were, and say why not?" Be the one who asks "why not?" Challenge yourself to think of positive things and then be innovative. This can apply in your business life or your personal life. This does not mean you will be able to make them happen, and certainly they may not be achieved without sacrifice. But if the dream or vision is truly worth doing, then the sacrifices are likely to be worth it.

BE HONORABLE—HAVE A MORAL COMPASS

Be guided by honorable thoughts and follow those thoughts with actions. Be truthful in your dealings with people. Have the courage to say no if that is appropriate. Don't tell folks you'll do something if you know there is not a chance you will be able to complete it. This applies to the personal and the professional. The folks you are honest with will respect you.

BE RESPECTED

Respect feeds on being honorable. I always had a goal of being respected by my friends, my professional colleagues, and my peers in the racing community. I just wanted to be open and honest with folks and have them respect me for treating them respectfully. This is how things ought to work. People do not always have to agree; they just need to be treated with respect.

LEARN AND GROW IN EVERYTHING YOU DO

Everyone should want to grow in life. Every day, learn something new and different. Understand that you can learn from a wide variety of perspectives and people. Someone once told me a checkbook full of people is more important than a checkbook full of money. I have always found this to be true. The more folks I meet and know, the greater my opportunity to learn from them. I will only stop learning when I stop breathing. Set your standards high and you will achieve high standards.

LOVE AND ENJOY WHAT YOU DO

The best thing we can experience is to love whatever it is that fills our time every day—whether that's work or something else. I have been fortunate in life. As a consultant, I could create new products and services and I liked what I did. If I didn't like the specific task, I liked the people I was doing it with or for. I felt fulfilled when I finished work and arrived home to my wife and daughters. Was it great every day? No. But I felt fulfilled and that's what spurred me on. The best thing was discovering that I could make enough money doing something I loved to do. However, it wasn't always like that. It took time, risk, and sacrifices to get there before those other things appeared. They weren't the objective—they just happened.

WORK WITH AND BE SURROUNDED BY PEOPLE YOU LIKE—AND LIKE TO BE WITH

This goes hand-in-hand with some of the other items here. The more folks you meet, the better position you'll be in to work with folks you like to be with. Do not be with folks you do not enjoy being with. In work, you frequently need to work together, but you should only deepen your involvement with folks you enjoy. Be selective in this regard.

BE GOOD AT WHAT YOU DO

If you strive to be excellent at what you do, then you will feel fulfilled and you will garner the respect of others. This does not mean only doing the things at which you excel. You must evolve in these things, and if you work hard you will excel. Mike Vance taught me that you can't retire. He said on one of the "Creative Leadership System" CDs that life is a process and you either live it from beginning to end or you don't. He also said that if you quit life or retire, you should forfeit all the chips you've accumulated. Mike believed that those who achieve things in life are the producers in our society. Once you achieve success, you have an obligation to assist others to be successful, thereby expanding the base of successful people in society and improving it. To accomplish this, the producers can't just retire.

Someone once asked me why I don't retire. I responded, "What I just heard you say is that I know more than I've ever known, know more people than I've ever known, make more money than

I've ever made, and so I should just quit?" That made no sense to me. I have to stay in the game. You must aim for a lifetime of continuous leaning and evolving. Mike would say there is only one time when you stop leaning and that's when you're dead.

I'm still going and will continue as long as I can. I am contributing—you should too. It feels really great.

HAVE PATIENCE

You also have to learn to have patience. It's a virtue. There is an old saying: "All things come to he who waits." When I was younger, I was very impatient and wanted to go, go, go. It's like in racing—we always want to go to throttle. But we shouldn't until it's time and the car is ready for it. The same is true in our lives. If we are impatient, we put too much pressure on ourselves and things tend not to work out, or we make more problems than we solve. I'm not saying wait for something to happen—quite the reverse. You need to take control and make things happen for yourself. Just recognize that you cannot become impatient, because life processes can take time to line up. Then you go to throttle and act.

48

Final Quotes

"If a person has no dreams, they no longer have any reason to live."

Ayrton Senna

"Anyone who stops learning is old—whether this happens at twenty or at eighty. Anyone who keeps on learning not only remains young but becomes constantly more valuable—regardless of physical capacity."

Henry Ford

In the movie *Dead Poets Society*, Robin Williams's character was teaching his class about life. He said we are all a part of a big book that's being written and each of us gets to write a chapter. The question he addressed to each member of the class was, "What are you going to write in your chapter?"

Personally, I take this a step further. When folks ask me why I don't relax and tell me to stop working so hard, my response is, *"I'm still writing my chapter."*

Keep writing YOUR chapter!

APPENDIX A

Exercise Regimens

WARNING: Ask your physician *before* undertaking this or any exercise program.

BASIC EXERCISE

Start with a low number of repetitions even if only one at first, then slowly progress.

Treadmill – 10–20 minutes

Dumbbell curls – 10 pounds, 30 reps x 2

Dumbbell side lifts 10 pounds, 30 reps x 2

Bands – light gray – extensions and curls – 30 reps x 2

Incline push-ups – 50 reps

One armed push-ups one hand on #6 medicine ball – 20 reps each side

Medicine ball #6 trunk rotations – 60 reps

Kettle weight lunges – 15pounds – 20 x 2

Bent leg sit-ups – 25 reps

Bent leg crunches – 25 reps

High plank – 2 x 1 min

Crunches – 3 x 30

Jumping jacks – 25

Low plank – 2 x 1 min

Wall sits – 100 count

Floor stretches – 2 min

LIMITED TIME EXERCISE USING BODY WEIGHT

10 minutes on treadmill

50 incline push-ups

25 lunges

50 air squats

1 minute – high plank

25 sit-ups

1 min – low plank

25 crunches

15-20 step-ups

25 jumping jacks

15 burpees

NOTE: One can begin with a limited number of repetitions for each exercise or by doing each exercise for a limited number of repetitions or seconds, as tolerated. Once tolerance and strength evolve, the repetitions and time can be increased. You may allocate the time evenly or differentially. Remember that form is important.

APPENDIX B

Priorities, Focus, and Gratitude

In my work and in my racing, I focus on what is most important. I usually have a lot of things on my plate. I rely on lists to prioritize and sometimes the lists get confusing and overwhelming. I tell folks if they ask me to do something and I tell them I will do it, they need to make sure I write it down. If it gets on the list, there is a reasonable chance it will get done. What follows is the process I use to getting things done.

PRIORITIES

I review the items on my list in the context of what must get done and what is most important. I do this for the month, week, and day. I review the list of the day and set priorities for what is most important on the list for that day. Generally, there are four or five important things. Once I get this done, I also review the list for what is needed to complete the items. For example, do I need anything from anyone else? If so, I add that to the list to get that working. And while that is working, I work on another item on the list if I need to wait for something. In this manner, I always have something to do.

FOCUS

Through the process above, I review the items and prioritize them. Then I only focus on the item that I have selected to complete first. I work on that item until it is completed. Of course, I can shift to another item if I run into a hang-up. Once the hang-up is resolved, I switch back to the initial priority item. I work my way down my list. Through this process, I am always busy, but I tend to achieve more.

GRATITUDE

When the work seems to get overwhelming, I reflect on the positives in my life and remind myself that I should be thankful for what I have and where I am. There are many who do not have work or do not earn as much as I do. This reflection allows me to place the bad things in context and when I do those negative things become "not so bad."

ACKNOWLEDGMENTS

The observations in *Focus Forward* are a byproduct of my thirty-two years of racing and my seventy-seven years of living.

While I can't recognize the many different individuals who have shaped my outlook on life, the racing material I discuss has been informed by years of experience with my co-drivers:

- Hugh Plumb
- Owen Trinkler
- Matt Plumb
- Mark Hamilton Peters
- Guy Cosmo
- David Murry

Without their coaching, support, encouragement, and friendship, I would not have been able to reach my current level of performance, nor endure for as long as I have. I have learned from all of them in different ways and I continue to do so.

I am also grateful for the support given to me by members of the TGM crew through the years.

Matt Rees also delivered valuable editorial guidance in the writing of *Focus Forward*.

ABOUT THE AUTHOR

TED GIOVANIS has been competing in road racing for more than three decades and began his professional career in 2006, at the age of 61.

Today, he is the owner of Team TGM and he races in the International Motor Sports Association series. He has competed throughout the United States and Europe, including 24 Hours of Daytona and the Ferrari Challenge in Monza, Italy. In 2020, he clinched the International GT Championship. He is the previous record-holder at Nelson Ledges road course in Ohio.

Ted is the founder of the Jayne Koskinas Ted Giovanis (JKTG) Foundation, which funds innovative medical research, data analysis, events, and other projects. In 2023, Johns Hopkins University launched the Giovanis Institute, which is focused on identifying the cellular strategies and molecular mechanisms driving cancer metastasis; developing countermeasures that prevent and disrupt metastasis; and changing the culture and practice of basic scientific research from "safe" investigation toward inquiry that welcomes high-value risk and stimulates innovation.

Ted is the award-winning author of *Beyond Fear: How I Fought the Feds for Six Years—and Won*. The book recounts how he overcame long odds to prevail in his lawsuit against the federal government, resulting in one of the largest court settlements in the history of Medicare.